AMAZING
GRACE NEWTON
and THE PURPLE PUDDLE

AMAZING
GRACE NEWTON
and THE PURPLE PUDDLE

N. JANE QUACKENBUSH

For information regarding permission, write to:
Attention: Hidden Wolf Books
155 West Genung St., St. Augustine, FL 32086

Copyright © 2018 by N. Jane Quackenbush
All rights reserved.
Published in the United States by Hidden Wolf Books.

ISBN 9780999434505
Library of Congress Control Number: 2018949970

Text set in Adobe Garamond

.

Version 1.1
Printed in the United States of America
First edition paperback printed, June 2018

To my family and friends.

Special thanks to
Kika Iadanza for her laser beams,
Joan Pospichal-LeBoss for rereading,
and my beautiful mother for her everything.

To: Clara

Stay Amazing!

∞ *One* ∞

The Grandfather Clock

The grandfather clock struck 11 AM, but the darkened sky reported otherwise. An angry plum-colored storm had passed, leaving a trail of electricity still live in the air, as I hurried to my special apple tree. My in-line skates made it nearly impossible to run, but my glittery fairy wings flapped just in time to keep me from falling.

I had to get out of the house. It was too loud

with Papa's football game reruns blaring in the background and Momma's awful crying. I was suffering from a hurt so strong but struggled to name or understand the feeling. Sometimes, it's hard to find a clear pathway through a fog of confusion.

I just knew whatever the feeling was, was bad. That's why I had to get to my twinkling tree (that's my special apple tree)—actually it was Nana's *and* my special apple tree. Down the cobbled path just beyond the rarely used old-fashioned well, the tree stood.

Minutes ago, I was upstairs skating around on the hard wooden floors chasing my masked little brother, Abel, who was wearing his usual ratty old towel around his neck pretending that it was a cape. Some of the trim had come loose on one end of the towel so he used it as a loop to wrap around his neck.

My momma had been hanging the damp laundry on the outside clothesline after the storm had passed. The next minute my momma had screamed. She screamed like never before then crumpled to the ground. We could see her from my upstairs bedroom window. Abel and I looked at each other, stopping our game. My papa was standing nearby and grabbed her hands to hold her, but she stayed on the ground wailing. I rolled down the hallway then scampered down the dark, spirally, carved-out stairs to hear the worst news of my life.

My nana had died.

My papa had found her.

My momma was sad.

I was confused.

✑ *Two* ✑

The Apple Tree

Nana and I had spent many days and evenings at the foot of this tree as the sun went down behind the mountains, watching fireflies flicker from here to there, telling it our secrets. So when I heard the news about her death, there was only one place I could think to go.

I sat under the tree's reaching branches, covered in leaves and fruit, as tears rolled down my burning cheeks. I pushed them away as quickly as I could. I didn't like the way they felt.

For no particular reason, I nervously rolled my flannel polka dot pajama bottoms up around my ankles.

To my nana, I was special. She loved me a lot. It seemed that she loved me more than anyone else in the world ... but I think everyone thought that same thing because I never knew a more popular person, ever. Everywhere we went, people stopped to talk to her, always leaving them with a smile, especially me. *What would I do without her*? I silently asked the tender trunk until I heard a stirring behind me. Maybe it was that apple that had fallen to the ground, now rolling? I wondered what made it drop.

I thought it might be the neighbor boys from the farm down the hill, Smith and Wesson. I looked around into the thicket of trees that bordered our farm expecting to see them wandering up as usual, but saw no one, and nothing moved. I heard it again and looked in the other direction where I saw a purple puddle filled with the morning's rain. It was reflecting the sky's dramatic storm that was passing by. A glittery sparkle danced on the water like a fairy. What was that? Was it a firefly? It was too early for them, I decided.

I wiped my tears away, sniffed up my snuggies (that's what my Nana called snot), and slowly crawled over to the puddle.

At first, I saw only my reflection—my springy strawberry-blonde hair, muddled brown eyes, my missing front tooth, my new jagged crooked tooth growing in, and the sixteen freckles on my cheeks and nose. I knew there were sixteen freckles because I counted them every day. And today I still had sixteen. Last month I had fourteen but two more had popped up one morning. My nana said that an angel must have kissed me two times in one night!

One of my leftover tears fell into the puddle and made rings that rippled to the edges. When the water was still again, I saw a smiling face reflecting back at me. I thought it was mine at first but knew that *I couldn't* be smiling.

"Hi there!" the puddle said.

"Huh?" I was stunned. How did the puddle talk?

"Who are you?" I asked.

"I'm Mazie."

I stared at the face in the puddle trying to understand how it could be that a puddle was talking to me.

"Why are you sad?" the puddle asked.

I *was* sad, but how did the puddle know? I guess it must have seen me crying. I sniffed and said, "I'm sad because my nana died. Now, I'll never, ever get to see her again." New tears welled up as the words I spoke re-broke my heart.

"Oh dear, that is sad. It's never easy losing someone you love, especially your nana," the puddle, I mean, Mazie, said comfortingly.

After a minute of silence, Mazie said, "How about you tell me all about her?"

I thought it was strange to talk to a puddle, but I couldn't think of anything better to do besides fidget with the wheels on my skates, rolling them around and around. So, I decided to go for it. At first I didn't know where to begin, but once I got the ball rolling, it kept on going.

"Well, *my* nana was always wearing an apron

and a smile. She baked the best chocolate chip cookies and the warmest panekakas (those are the most delicious, extra tasty, special pancakes my nana made). I could eat them every day of my whole life. They never got old—just like Nana. In fact, she never got tired or grey. Her silvery hair looked like it was spun from moon dust. It went down to her waist when it was loose but she mostly wore it looped in buns all around her head. She had deep blueberry eyes that crinkled in the corners, especially when she smiled, which was all the time. And she never complained. She was too busy smiling."

"How did she die? Was she sick?"

I put my finger up to my chin and thought about how to answer Mazie. "I never knew my nana to be sick. I guess she was older, but she never let her age hold her back from doing what she wanted. She could do anything! Because she said so. And that's what she would say. She would say, *I can do anything because I said so!*"

Mazie's face looked excited about my stories so I went on. "By anything, I mean, she could cook the biggest Thanksgiving dinners, sew the neatest stitches, plant the richest gardens, and she even danced every day of her life. She would say, *Life's a dance! You can sit out or find the dance floor and boogie.* My nana boogied."

Mazie giggled. I smiled, remembering my nana's moves. Her head would tilt back and her eyes would close, when she was really feeling the music.

I figured she would ask me about my pop pop so I went ahead and told her about him.

"Pop Pop died before I was born, but I felt like I knew him since my nana always talked about him like he was still alive. They were married for forty blissful years *and one **extra happy one**,* she'd always say. Anytime something reminded her of him, she would tell me a story; that made it so I got to know him. When I would see pictures of them dancing or photos of just him on his favorite tractor, I imagined what he was like."

"That's sweet," Mazie said.

"Nana was my momma's momma. *My* momma doesn't dance through life. She kind of sits out and watches everyone else having fun. I think momma secretly does want to dance, but she said many times that all *those people looked silly havin' too much fun and doin' who knows what* ... I think my momma would be happier if she danced."

"I think the whole world would be happier if they danced!" Mazie said as she twirled around in the puddle singing some silly song.

For a minute there, I forgot that I was sad when I caught myself smiling.

"Get up and dance with me," Mazie said.

"Now?"

"If not now, when?" she asked.

I couldn't think of an answer so I got up to dance while Mazie hummed a tune that sounded tender, fun, and silly all at once.

"What are you doing?" Hope, my older sister, asked.

"Huh?" I almost screamed because she had snuck up on me.

"Are you really dancing at a time like this? Don't you even care that Nana died?" Hope wasn't much of a smiler, in fact, she was an expert on looks of disappointment. I was used to them by now, but the look she gave me made me feel awful about myself.

The expression on her face was one of

disgust mixed with bewilderment. Hope was five years older than I but seemed to act more like twenty years older. Of course I cared that Nana had died, but somehow talking to Mazie had made that hurt less painful. I thought maybe Mazie could help Hope, too, so I said, "Hope, I'd like you to meet my new friend." I scooted Hope over to the puddle.

Hope looked around for a human then followed my stare and asked, "Is this puddle your new friend?" She said this sarcastically, at first, but then examined my face for verification.

I didn't know what to say because even I, at my tender age of seven, knew that having a puddle as your friend sounded nuts.

AND THE PURPLE PUDDLE

৶ *Three* ৶

Hope

"I swear Grace, sometimes you can be so juvenile," Hope scoffed at me. "You really should behave more appropriately. Our nana has just died, and all you can think to do is dance around with an imaginary puddle?" She held her hands up indicating my childish way of dealing with death. But I didn't know any better. Plus, the purple puddle didn't appear imaginary to me, it looked real, as did Mazie.

What are you supposed to do when you lose your best and only nana? No one I knew had died, not even a pet. They went on to *greener pastures*, as Papa used to say. When my gerbil, Herman, went to greener pastures, I was kind of sad but kind of not sad *because he was in a better place,* that's what Papa had said. When my goldfish, Smithers, went to live in the big blue ocean, I imagined him finding a big school of fish to join. He'd never be lonesome again.

But I was so very lonesome until Papa brought home Noodle, my pet chicken. He was just a chick, and he fit inside my palm. Actually, he was nearly the same size as my hand and bright yellow, like a cheesy macaroni noodle.

I wasn't sure how Hope thought I *should* behave so I went to look for Abel to see how *he* was behaving. I found him in his little room filled with plaques and banners of superheroes.

He had a set of built-in bunk beds, but he used the bottom bunk as his "**LAIR**", (that means superhero hideout). It was covered in old quilts and blankets that draped over from the top bunk. Inside he had a lighted spinning globe so he would know where to go when his super heroic aid was needed.

Papa was kneeling down in front of Abel, on top of his colorful alphabet rug, telling him something I couldn't hear. Abel looked sad but seemed to take the news okay. Papa used Abel's cape, I mean towel, to wipe away some of his own tears.

Papa sniffed then said, "We will miss her very much, but one day we'll see her again in the afterlife."

So that's where she was, Nana was in the "afterlife". My brain paused on that thought. I wondered what the afterlife looked like. I imagined the ocean where Smithers had gone with big blue whales blowing bubbles that floated all the way up to Heaven. Then I thought of big wide meadows with rainbows everywhere and a cloud forest filled with waterfalls that were falling into forever. The afterlife didn't seem so bad.

"And one day, after we've lived a full life here, we'll all be together again," my papa assured Abel.

❧ *Four* ❧
Church

The morning of Nana's funeral, my momma dressed us up fancy, like we were heading to church. I wasn't allowed to wear my wings, safety gear, polka dot flannels, or my inline skates. Momma was wearing a color that I wasn't used to seeing her in, black. Papa was in his fancy grey suit. It was the same one he had worn when my parents were married. He was so proud that he could still fit into it after all these years.

I was told to wear the fancy dress that Nana had made for me. I didn't mind; it reminded me of her. It was light blue with a drop waist. Puffy sleeves capped my shoulders with an elastic band that encircled my upper arm. Little ruffles in a square surrounded three brass buttons around the chest area. I looked at myself in the full-length mirror and felt proud and mature until I was struggling with the tights Momma had laid out for me on her bed. I was tipping over to the left or crashing into the laundry basket to the right, not making very much progress.

"Here Grace, let me help you." Momma bent over while I placed my feet in the openings as she helped me wiggle into the tight white stockings.

Ohhhh! Here's the best part—I got to wear my noisy shoes that my Nana had given to me last Christmas. They were black patent leather Mary Jane's that clicked and clacked on our wooden floors.

Click Clack Click Clack Click Clack …

I liked the way they sounded, so I made excuses to hear them.

Click Clack Click Clack Click Clack …

I tapped them until my mother asked me (actually told me—in a loud way) to stop that *INCESSANT STOMPING*.

Poop ...

My older sister, Hope, was still getting ready. She had on her dark pink, ruffly dress that tied in a big bow on the back. After she was all dressed, Momma curled Hope's long, straight, dark hair while my dad was wrestling with Abel to get cleaned up. Abel was regularly a mess and Hope was always so neat whereas I was somewhere in the middle. Guess that's why I found myself outside waiting for them to be ready. It also gave me an excuse to spend my spare time next to the puddle.

"Don't you look nice!" Mazie said.

"Why, thank you!" I said as I spun around almost losing my balance because I got a little dizzy. "Whoa!" I recovered before I fell into the puddle. My momma would have lost her mothballs if I had fallen into a puddle and ruined my nice dress, white stockings, and patent leather shoes!

Right after I thought that, Momma's voice called out, "Grace! Grace! Where are you?" I looked over to our treehouse and saw everyone spilling out from the front porch. Everyone was ready to go.

I started to go but then looked back at the puddle, ready to explain that I had to go … but Mazie wasn't there anymore. That was strange, I thought. I slowly walked away wondering why she always disappeared when I walked away. But then I thought it might be strange to ever have seen her. A girl who looked almost just like me that lived inside a puddle?

AND THE PURPLE PUDDLE

⨾ *Five* ⨿

The Pickup Truck

The heavy doors on Papa's old red pickup truck closed loudly. With a couple of groans and a thump, he cranked up the loud, gurgly engine. It smelled musty mixed with old gasoline inside the truck, even with the windows down—for some reason, I liked it.

As we got to the bottom of the hill, I looked at the faded sign that had a big apple tree carved into the wood with letters that read, "Newton's

Apple Farm". The sign was nestled between two flowering bushes to the right of the driveway.

On the way to the funeral, all five of us sat in the bouncy vinyl front seat. Momma sat next to Papa who drove, Hope sat next to Momma, Abel sat on Hope's lap, and I sat next to the window, thoughtlessly picking at a rust scab on the door. I liked looking out.

We were a little cramped but because we were small, (us kids, that is), we fit. The rusty, old truck sputtered along the country road until we got to the little white parish that Nana and Pop Pop had attended forever.

We used to attend more regularly when I was younger, but now we only came here on special occasions like Easter and Christmas to watch Nana sing in the choir. She had a harmonious voice, like a nightingale that echoed into the green valley along the country roads.

As I was walking up, I noticed the tall steeple and the bell tower, the wooden double doors, and the big stone steps that led to a front porch where people greeted one another.

Two boys noticed me as I made my way toward the entry. Smith and Wesson, the neighbor boys, were looking at me while hiding snickering smirks behind their hands. They weren't used to seeing me all dressed up. Most days when we played together, I wore old, worn-out shorts and t-shirts, not dresses.

Smith and Wesson were twins, *but* they looked nothing alike. One was red-headed with freckles, and the other had dark hair and skin to match. They looked nothing like brothers, but they shared the same country accents.

My feet crunched on the gravel as Abel raced past me with my dad following him in hot pursuit. Even though Abel wasn't allowed to wear his cape today, it didn't stop him from being *super*. Smith and Wesson skittered along with Abel while I stayed behind. I didn't want to mess up my special dress on such an important occasion.

… I smelled powder and perfume.

Old ladies with a spectrum of rainbow-colored hair took turns hugging my momma. They all swooned over Hope and her long, dark curls. Because I wasn't sensational like Hope evidently was, as a consolation, the old ladies tried to make me feel better by squeezing my cheeks.

It didn't help.

The perfume became so strong that my head began to ache.

"Just look at all those freckles you have!" one powdery, old, purple-haired lady said to me as she held my chin. She had brown teeth and even browner lines between each tooth. Chalky makeup which had to be an inch thick was masking her humanity.

At first I thought she liked my "angel kisses" … until she said to my mother, "Ruth, honey, there's this new product I can get for her to make those wretched spots disappear, you know. In fact, I actually sell it!" She said this as if she too was surprised by the happenstance.

She handed my momma a pamphlet, got right next to her while spinning her head around in my momma's face, and said, "Ruth, these products are 100% all natural and are set at very competitive prices as they are … *BUT* … if you want the best discount *and* make some money on the side, you can start selling these products, too!"

Momma backed away. The excitement this lady was trying to spread was not contagious but that didn't stop her from trying to be infectious. "Cary Mae is the name of the company." She could sense that she was losing Momma's attention so she redirected her to the prize. "Oh, and Ruth, dear, do you see that lavender beauty over yonder in the parking lot?" She pointed to a large, light purple, boat-sized car. "Would you believe that I earned enough money from Cary Mae to put a down payment on it? It is very luxurious, I know … Plus, it matches my beautiful hair color, wouldn't you say?"

Momma wasn't interested in this lady's business proposal or her products, it seemed, but this lady wouldn't give up so easily. "Tell you what, Ruth," she pulled Momma over to tell her something so that no one but I could hear. "With the gravity of the situation, I don't want to talk about business at a funeral for your mother," she whispered.

"Oh, good, yes, thank you, Dottie," my momma said with relief washing over her already grieving face.

"How about I stop by when all the dust has settled?"

Momma looked shocked and a little confused. "Um, we'll have to see. I'm not ..."

The lady cut her off and said, "Shhhhhh! Not now, dear!" She followed her statement with a little wink then whispered, "We'll talk later." She looked at me as she muttered, "Stubborn little rascals those freckles are, you poor little girl, helpless, I tell you." A brown smile snuck up on her face when she said, "But I can help ... Dottie Doohinkley can help... so don't you worry. We'll talk later, okay?"

AND THE PURPLE PUDDLE

ꝏ *Six* ꝏ

Stained Glass Windows

Inside the red carpeted church, stained-glass windows shone beams of purple, ruby, amber, and other jewel-toned light to color our grief-stricken faces. I could see a long wooden box in the front of the church with one of its two lids open. People took turns to look inside. When it was my turn, I saw a body that resembled Nana's, but her makeup was all wrong. The lipstick was too pink, and there was no beauty mark. Her hair was combed weird, and her skin was an ashy color.

Normally, Nana's skin was a warm tanned color from all her gardening, and when she wore lipstick, it was a dark raspberry red color. Nana didn't have to do much to look pretty, I guess that's why she didn't look right; they had used too much makeup.

After the mourners had a chance to say their goodbyes, everyone sang a song that had my name at the beginning. I had heard Nana sing this song many times, even when she wasn't in church. I listened as the whole congregation sang together …

Amazing Grace, how sweet the sound …

My papa looked over at me and gave me a big, tear-filled wink. Momma sang along with tears in her eyes, too. I had to look away when her chin began to quiver. I grabbed her empty hand and held it to my cheek hoping my tears would be stopped by her touch. Hope stood like a steadfast soldier while Abel was under the pew drawing stick figures on the bottom of the seat.

On our way out, a gentleman named Mr. Skwertz who owned and ran the local dairy farm, shook Papa's hand but he wanted to talk to Momma, in particular.

"I sure am sorry to hear about Andromeda. Your mother was a comet ... out of this world, I tell ya. I'd had my eye on her for years, but she had only one spot in her heart for a man, and that was forever taken by Luther, your daddy. Luther was a good man ... my best friend, in fact ... all through high school, but when he married Andromeda, I had to let the two of 'em go. I had to keep a respectful distance so as not to intrude on a sacred oath. But when Luther died, I thought I had a chance ... but nope. Was never to be. But that didn't stop me from tryin'—*coot coot*," he chortled before nudging Papa.

With a little snort he continued, "By the way, I'd like you to meet my grandson, Tater. His real name is Matteo but I don't speak Spanish, so I called him Tater and well, Tater Skwertz just has a certain ring to it, so it just stuck."

Tater looked over at me and sincerely said,

"I'm sorry. I … I know the loss you're feeling, too." Out of the blue, Tater leaned over and gave me a hug. That was nice, I thought, but very unexpected. Right after he finished hugging me, he looked up at his grandfather, gave Momma and Papa a nod, and then led the old man, Mr. Skwertz, away.

I couldn't wait to leave. Even though the church was very pretty and looked peaceful, Nana wasn't in this place, I knew it. I couldn't wait to get back home to my twinkling tree and puddle. I felt Nana's spirit there.

AND THE PURPLE PUDDLE

৶ Seven ৶

The Treehouse

We Newtons lived in a thousand-year-old house made out of a hollowed-out oak tree stump. It wasn't your average big ole oak tree, this one was wider, rounder, and taller than most people's entire cabins around here. The heart of our home was the towering gnarled stump. Through the years, additions and lean-tos were added as necessary ... like when a new baby arrived. Momma had planted trellises of flowering vines that climbed up the sides and over the roof making our house look alive. Yellow jessamine flowers bloomed alongside purple wisteria. Coral colored honeysuckles provided a sweet snack, while wild climbing hydrangeas sprouted high into the sky giving our house a lovely, bright canopy. Our whimsical treehouse was surrounded by green hills, tall trees, trickling streams, colorful cows, and smoky mountains.

Our farm was small compared to the other ones around us but it sustained us plentifully. We grew apples on big, bountiful trees. They were the sweetest apples you could ever bite into. They had a rich crunch and a sweet tart flavor that made them perfect for pies, sauce, and applejack (I wasn't allowed to have that, but that's what I was told). I liked the apples best off the tree with the skin still crisp from the morning dew.

I was crunching on one when I heard the same sound that I had heard the other day. I had a hunch so I walked over to the puddle.

"Hi Mazie!"

"Hi! You seem happy today."

I wasn't sure if I should "seem" happy considering how Hope had made me feel guilty for not looking sad enough. I missed Nana *a lot*. I felt bad, but I wasn't sure how long I was supposed to be sad.

"Well, I … uh …" I stuttered.

"Grace, you don't have to be sad forever. You're allowed to feel happy," Mazie said.

"But Momma is still sad and I don't know how to make her happy. She cries a lot. Day and night, I hear her. Papa doesn't know what to say. He just takes Abel to his soccer games to get him out of the way. You know how boys are," I explained in my most adult-sounding explanation.

"Oh, yes, boys are a whole lot of energy wrapped up in a ball of gas," Mazie burbled.

I remembered Nana saying something just like that one time. I wondered if Mazie had heard her say it, too. "My nana said stuff like that."

"I know. I heard her. She told me about your mother, how she was one of the prettiest girls in all of Apple Valley. I heard all about your father, how he was a dashing young football player bound for the big leagues until the war drafted him and stole his promising career; how Hope is the legacy your mother is living through; and how Abel is your father's chance to relive his glory days."

I wondered what Nana had said about me. Without me asking, Mazie said, "As far as you were concerned, she said you were *AMAZING*."

"Amazing?" I asked.

"Yes, she said you were *AMAZING*," Mazie said again in an extended tone that sounded … actually, *AMAZING*.

"How?" I asked.

"How what?"

"How am I amazing?"

"If you don't know now, you will. Just believe me. It's better that way."

Mazie sounded so much like Nana that I had to look again. Nope, she wasn't Nana, but I guess when you spend a lot of time around someone, you start to sound like them.

৶ *Eight* ৶

The Kitchen

"Grace! I need you to come in here and help me with these dishes," Momma called. I hated doing dishes, but I loved my momma so I went in to help.

Momma was standing in front of our large white porcelain sink. An open window above the sink gave Momma a clear view to her garden. The window was framed with little buttercup curtains blowing from the breezes outside. She stared out, getting lost in her thoughts. Momma's long wavy, brown hair was up in a sloppy bun; she was pretty even though she looked sad, but she was especially lovely when she was happy.

"I need you to dry these dishes as I wash them, please," she said.

"Okay, Momma."

"Thank you, Grace."

Momma was always grateful, but, recently, she seemed worn out. Not even Noodle, who pecked and poked around, cleaning up after her, cheered her up.

"Momma, guess what?" I asked.

Momma exhaled. "Grace, I don't have the energy for this. Can it wait?" she said with a deflated expression, almost like she was ready to cry.

Upsetting Momma was the last thing I wanted to do so I stayed quiet even though I wanted to tell her about Mazie ... how she reminded me of Nana ... how she could go visit Mazie, too and maybe make herself feel better. But I guess it could wait. Maybe I would save it for a real special occasion.

I picked up wet plates while using a dishtowel to wipe them before placing them in our wooden cabinets that my Papa had made with his own hands. I needed a step stool for the higher shelves.

Crash!

Noodle flapped his wings and ran for cover.

A couple of unwashed tea cups fell to the hard wood floor. Momma somehow dropped them. When I looked at her face, I saw tears filling her eyeballs, but I didn't think she was upset about her broken dishes.

I tried to help her clean up.

"Grace, I need you to just please stay out of the way." Her tone hurt my feelings. All I wanted to do was help make her feel better, but I guess nothing would.

Momma looked over at me then changed her expression. "I'm sorry, Grace. It's not your fault. I just don't want you to get hurt."

"Don't worry, Momma, I'll be extra careful."

Momma was muttering some gibberish as she was sweeping up the broken dishes but all I could make out was, "Dang gravity".

❧ • ❧

After I finished helping Momma, I found Hope in her room doing homework. Hope was studying to become a record-breaking astronaut, and her room was filled with posters of astronauts like John Glen and Alan Shepard, but her favorite was Sally Ride—the first American woman in space. I knew that because Hope had always talked about Sally and all the studies she had to do in order to achieve her mission.

In the spots where there were no posters, Hope's room had shelves stuffed with books about outer space. They had detailed pictures in them of stars and words that I had a hard time reading and pronouncing, but Hope would always correct me. I loved looking into outer space, but my career aspirations weren't set so loftily. I wanted to help people—help them feel better. Doing stuff for others often, almost always, made me feel better, too.

"Hi Hope!" I said before Hope raised her head up from her thick book.

"Grace, do you mind? I'm right in the middle of studying for a huge, very important … test … And if I don't pass, I will be doomed."

An exam in the summer? That sounded icky. "What's dang gravity?"

"Dang gravity?" she wondered. "I'm not sure if there are other kinds of gravity other than the force that attracts objects to the earth."

"Where is it?" I asked.

"It's all around you."

I looked around but couldn't find it.

"No, silly. It's invisible but that doesn't mean that it's not there."

"Oh," I said, strangely understanding her.

Hope looked at me and then tried to make me leave with her silence. She dismissed me and went back to her book. I was glad to have Hope around to answer my questions when I was stumped.

"I can see it now, Apple Valley's own Hope Newton, record-breaking astronaut!" I said while pantomiming her name in lights on a banner across town.

She looked up and watched my hands as they invisibly lit up her name; Hope smiled.

✍ *Nine* ☙
Noodle

Next afternoon while I was dressing Noodle up in some old baby clothes, I heard Momma call my name, telling me that Smith and Wesson were here to play.

"Noodle, you just look so adorable! I'll be right back."

Noodle clucked.

I ran down and greeted the boys in my

normal, not fancy attire, then ran outside ahead of them after saying, "Hi! Smith. Hi! Wesson."

Their dad loved guns but Smith and Wesson did not.

Not long ago, Mr. Springfield, their dad, took them hunting. They were all excited about their first "real" "big boy" hunting trip. Their plans were set weeks ahead of time. They had talked about it non-stop; they were so excited. Their mother had helped prepare their outfits and gear for the long weekend in the deep dark woods.

Smith and Wesson and their dad stalked around in the timberland looking for an animal to shoot. Just to get some practice in before the big kill, Mr. Springfield had instructed them to shoot a little bushy-tailed squirrel. Wesson hit it square in the temple. It died and both boys cried so hard they refused to ever pick up another BB gun or rifle.

I remembered their momma telling my momma all about it over some coffee one morning.

"Oh, the irony!" they chuckled.

I didn't know what irony meant at the time.

I asked the twins about it, but I guess it meant an incident they didn't care to talk about.

Mr. Springfield tried everything he could think of besides tanning their hides to go back hunting with him, but their minds were set. It really bothered their father because Smith's and Wesson's aims were flawless. They could hit aluminum cans even with a slingshot from twenty yards away. I wasn't a bad shot either, usually.

We were having some target practice out in the driveway, knocking over lined-up cans along the fence when Smith said, "Dern, Grace what's wrong with you today? You got cobwebs in your eyeballs? You ain't hit but one can so far."

Poop …

I looked over at my cans knowing my heart wasn't into this activity but pulled myself together then dropped all eight cans in a row. I blew the invisible smoke off my slingshot as if it was a real pistol.

Smith's and Wesson's eyes grew. They looked impressed at my skills. I laughed because I, too, was impressed with myself but felt silly being overly bumptious. As dusk invited fireflies to blink here and there, Smith and Wesson knew that was their cue to *git on home*.

I took my time getting home because my house was filled with too much sadness. I looked up at the star-filled sky. Nature seemed unfazed by the death of my nana. As I was looking up, I twirled around making the sky look like it was spinning. The stars turned into circular lines as they connected to one another. I stopped only because I became too dizzy. Suddenly a star streaked across the sky. Were those leftover effects from my spinning? Or did it really happen?

"Grace!" I heard Papa call.

"Coming!"

I didn't have time to wonder anymore. I ran home to tell Papa all about my sharp shooting skills and possibly seeing a shooting star.

"Well, did you make a wish?" he asked while passing around Momma's homemade spaghetti.

"A wish?"

"Yeah! Don't you know that when you see a shooting star, you're supposed to make a wish?"

"Guess not," I said. "Will it come true? Whatever I wish for?"

"Well, there's only one way to find out," Papa said.

Hope chimed in, "Okay, *now* I see where Grace gets all of her delusions."

"What are duh-lusions?" Abel asked, looking like a clown with his mouth covered in red spaghetti sauce.

"Delusions are things that people make up that don't really exist, but wishes are different from delusions. Some would call wishes far-fetched desires, but I choose to call them hope for a brighter future," Papa said as he squeezed Momma's empty hand. Momma stayed quiet but gave him a soft smile. "And you know what I'm hoping for?" Papa asked.

"What?" Abel and I excitedly asked.

"That morning will come with not *too* much sun so we can get all those apples picked in time."

"Oh, can I help?" I asked.

Papa and Momma looked at one another and shrugged. "Sure can," Papa said then winked.

"Me too! Can I?" Abel offered.

"If you can get out of bed early enough," Papa said. "Gotta get started by 6 AM."

"Never mind, that's too early," Abel said frowning.

We all laughed at his silly down-turned, doubtful facial expression.

∾ *Ten* ∾

The Apple Orchard

All morning my papa and the picker crew were harvesting our Golden Early Apples. Lucky for me, I woke up in time to help. I climbed the ladders, picking bushels and bushels of juicy chartreuse apples. I wanted to sneak a bite out of a few extra juicy-looking ones but restrained myself. Some of the more reluctant stinkers made it so I had to pull hard in order for them to be picked, but, eventually, even the stubborn fruit gave way.

Papa picked the apples like a pro, of course. Sweat marks covered his white t-shirt as his muscled arms plucked the fruit effortlessly. He was the strongest man in the universe. My papa could beat up anyone and everyone, all at the same time. I just knew it ... not that anyone ever challenged him to a brawl. Everyone must have known better. He had that look in his eye—that *don't mess with me* look. But he never gave that look to me or my momma or my family. He saved a special look for us—a look of love. He'd do anything for us.

Under a canopy of fruit-filled trees, Papa said, "Grace, you are a fine apple-picker," while we took a break for lunch. "I think you've picked more than these five grown men combined."

The grown men grunted with mouthfuls of sandwiches while I boastfully smiled. Momma had made my sandwich, but I had packed the rest of my lunch pail. I included a nectarine, a homemade sticky granola bar, and a huge, gooey, rich chocolatey brownie.

The guys were looking at my chunky brownie. *I* could understand. If someone else was eating this brownie, I would stare at it, too.

I couldn't eat it all by myself (actually I could) but it would be mean to not share so I broke off a couple of hunks and gave the men each a bite.

That would make them feel better.

By the way they worked in the second half of the day, I could tell that my brownie had helped. They were feeling better all right because we almost doubled the bushels from the morning, at least that's what Papa said.

After we finished and were walking back home, Papa was saying what he said after every harvest:

"For I have had too much of apple picking:
I am overtired
Of the great harvest I myself desired."

I liked the way that sounded and repeated it to myself over and over. As we got closer to the house, I noticed that we had picked from most all the trees in the orchard. But the apple tree closest to our house, the one that I called my special twinkling tree was not touched by any pickers, and *it* had the sweetest fruit.

All of the other trees had green apples, but the twinkling tree had bright red, heart-shaped apples ... maybe that's why it was so special.

It was also taller than the others and broader—its trunk, that much more sturdy. No wonder it was favored; it was a beautiful tree, and I had wished upon it.

As we were walking toward the tree, I asked, "How come we never sell the apples from this tree? Didn't you say that they were the sweetest ones?"

Papa stopped walking and turned to me to say, "Yes, I did say that, and yes they are. But look over there." I looked to where he was pointing. "Now look over there." He pointed to the left, and I saw a sea of apple orchards in all directions. "Those trees are for everyone else, but this tree is only for us. It's *OUR* tree," he said as he plucked an extra-tasty looking apple.

"Your Nana planted this tree when she moved over here. She also planted that whole garden over there." He pointed to the little vegetable garden my momma now tended.

"Who planted all the other apple trees?" I asked about the orchards.

"My papa did most of them. He did the one on the east side, and when I got home from the war, I planted the one on the west. Gave me something to do … to get my mind clear."

I knew Pop Pop and Nana were Momma's parents but I had never known my papa's parents. "Papa, where's your momma and papa?"

My papa looked hard into my eyes then looked away as they became a tad watery. "They died when I was off to war." He made a *piff* noise and shook his head. "Here I go across the world to help save some strangers, whose enemies wanted to kill *me* … worrying my parents *literally* to death. Here they were, with no hint of danger, no sign of threat, in the comfort of their own home, and there I was in the most dangerous situation with guns pointed at me from every direction, and I come out alive … and they die? Sheesh … I tell you, some things just don't make no sense."

My papa almost never talked about the war he had fought in, but I could tell from time to time that he was still fighting some kind of enemy in his head. He was a strong man, but Nana told me that even the strongest men can't un-see things.

"What were they like, your momma and

papa?" I asked, hoping that if he talked about his parents, it would help him feel better. But he shook his head and said, "It's been so long; I can hardly remember. But I can tell you one thing, you remind me of my mother—especially certain looks in your eyes. Makes me feel like a part of her lived on inside of you."

He looked into my eyes and smiled. Talking about them seemed to make him feel better, after all.

As we walked into the house, Abel was running around the kitchen and living room, making a zooming sound like he was a super-human machine. Papa laughed because he liked seeing Abel do his thing. Noodle was strutting back and forth in his overalls, following behind Momma as she was making dinner. Papa grabbed my momma and kissed her.

"Ruth?" His gesture surprised her but she played along.

"Yes, Lumen?"

"I got something for you."

"What is it?"

He pulled a ripe red apple from behind his back and put it in her hand. She held it, examined its color, squeezed it, put it up to her mouth, then bit into it.

"Do you like it?" he asked.

"Yes, but I don't have time for this," she said as she took another bite. As she bit, Papa leaned in and took a bite from the other side. She let him take the apple from her. She was obviously still sad. She must have known that the fruit was from Nana's tree.

I wanted to help my momma feel better but didn't know how. I wanted to console my papa who now looked hurt by Momma's rejection.

Abel came in screeching like a wild owl. Momma's eyes rolled before she turned back to her supper preparations.

"Grace, go get cleaned up for supper and ask Hope to come down here and set the table," Momma said.

"I'm here Momma," Hope said. I turned to see Hope with a stack of plates walking over to the kitchen table.

I volunteered, "I'll help you Hope, just as soon as I'm finished washing up."

✑ *Eleven* ✑

Dinnertime

The rustic, rectangular, white farm table was now set. Everyone gathered around, ready to eat.

Noodle clucked as we sat nibbling chicken casserole. The phone rang. Momma picked it up and talked to a person who sounded like a weird brass instrument. After a lot of *uh-huh's* and *okay's,* she hung up.

"Who was that?" Papa asked.

"That was Aunt Esther; she wants to come and help clean out Nana's cottage."

Nana had lived in a small wooden cottage at the bottom of our hill. My heart hurt every time we drove past it, unlit by the string of white lights that she kept up all year long. The first night I noticed the darkness of her shadowy cottage was on the way home from her funeral.

We all looked.

We all noticed.

We all were bothered by it.

After that, my Papa set her lights to illuminate on a timer so that even though Nana wasn't there anymore, her lights would still come on. Somehow that made Momma and all of us a bit happier.

Across the way from Nana's cottage, in a cleared meadow, was an old storage barn that doubled as Nana's boogie barn. Every Monday, Wednesday, and Saturday, loads of fancy-dressed ladies and one gentleman, Mr. Skwertz, showed up from across town to boogie with Nana for hours. If the wind was blowing right, we could hear the music thumping all the way up to our hillside house.

Sometimes if I hurried and got the dishes done early, Momma would let me go and dance with Nana and her friends. I wasn't as good as Nana who glided across the room like a trotting show pony, but I sure did have fun rootin' and scootin' with the ladies and gentleman.

I hadn't been inside her cottage since the day before she died. That day Nana and I had spent all morning making aprons from scraps of fabric. She sold them at the local farmer's market every weekend. Everyone loved the special little touches she included like a cut out of a gingerbread man hiding in the front pocket or a flower poking out from one of the side pockets. She put ruffles along the edges that wrapped around and tied into pretty bows on the back.

It was my job to thread the needles because her *old eyes could barely see a charging elephant anymore*, she had said. I also ironed all the scraps and lined them up for her to run through the sewing machine. Every once in a while, she would let me do the running, but I was a little scared to mess up her beautiful work. "You're really good at this," she'd say. "Very straight lines, I think you could do this all by yourself one day." Boy, did that make me feel proud. Nana was the best seamstress that ever existed, and for her to say something like that *to me*, made me beam.

As a reward for all of our labor, we baked cookies together. She made *THE* best chocolate chip cookies in the world. They were buttery, sugary, and chocolatey with just the right amount of yum. I would always sneak a few scoops of the irresistible uncooked batter. It would hold me over while pans dotted with dough were safely in the oven (away from my greedy hands).

Nana always had fresh milk from Mr. Skwertz's dairy farm up the hill. We would dunk the warm cookies into the ice cold milk before putting the dripping crumbles into our fortunate mouths.

Just in time, Abel and Papa had come in for an afternoon treat.

"Cookies!" Abel exclaimed.

"We followed our noses to the best smelling cabin in the mountains," Papa said.

"Well, pull up a chair and get to dunking!" Nana said as she filled a plate with warm cookies and poured iced-milk into blue mason jars.

Abel giggled as he ate. That's what he did when he really liked something. Momma had a hard time getting him to eat any "real" food, (like carrots, beans, actually, anything green, chicken, and whatever else that was wholesome), but when he found something that he liked to eat, he giggled. Papa just wanted Abel to grow big and strong so whatever Abel ate voluntarily was okay with him.

Nana smiled as she watched us enjoying her treat. She loved to spoil us, especially me, it seemed … at least that's what her twinkly wink told me.

Nana's hugs went all around when it was time for us to go on home. Abel let Nana hug him before he zoomed away in his cape (that old junky towel), and Papa gave Nana a kiss on the cheek before it was my turn. Nana gave the best hugs, and I didn't want mine to be rushed so I waited to be last. Her hugs cradled my whole body in warm garden scented dryer sheets. She reminded me of pillows that came to life because she was so soft and cuddly.

I looked up at her and smiled before I turned to go.

"Luf you!" she said. (That's how she said, "love you"). Nana looked sparkly as usual. I would never have guessed that she would die the next day.

✍ *Twelve* ✍
Photo Album

After brushing my teeth and getting ready to go night night, I walked into my lamp-lit room and found Papa sitting at the edge of my bed with a large open photo album. I bounced up next to him. I loved looking at pictures!

"What's this?" I asked. I looked at the old black and white photos.

Papa spoke softly, "Remember how you

were asking about my parents? Well, this is your Grandpa Ernest Newton and Grandma Pru Newton—my mother and father."

I looked at the pictures. A small, light-haired woman had her head resting on a strong-looking, dark-haired man's chest. They looked young and happy. I looked up at my papa and smiled. He smiled back.

"Here's me when I was a baby." He handed me a square photo with wavy edges. It smelled like an old cinnamon stick. His momma was holding a wrapped-up little baby while standing in front of a unique house. I looked at the wooden windows then noticed the Dutch door in the background.

"Hey, that's our house!" I exclaimed.

Papa grunted jovially, verifying my suspicion. "You're right! This ole treehouse and farm used to be theirs … and their parents before that."

We flipped through more pictures of my grandpa building new additions to our once much smaller home, pictures of him driving his old cars, riding horses, and even holding my papa on his lap when he was a toddler.

We looked through the whole album as Papa told me about each picture. I felt like I was able to get to know his momma and papa even though we had never met. The last picture in the book must have been taken just before they had died. It was a picture of my papa in his service uniform. Underneath the picture, there was what looked like an old water droplet. Papa rubbed it as a fresh tear drop fell next to it.

"Don't cry, Papa!" I said trying to spread my smile over to him. It seemed to work because he smiled back and sniffed up his tears. He closed the photo album and gave me hug.

"Mind if I tuck you into bed tonight?" he asked.

"Uh-uh," I said as he helped me under the covers. I pulled my patchwork quilt up to my chin. He made a long, overly unnecessary display of tucking my blankets around and under every inch of my body. He gave me a little tickle, and then he pretended to shush me when I giggled too loud. Papa was silly sometimes.

"Good night, Grace," he said as he turned off the lamp on my bedside table.

"Good night, Papa," I said as he and his shadow walked away.

❧ *Thirteen* ❧

New Bikes

Aunt Esther was set to arrive the next morning to help Momma clean and organize Nana's cottage. It never looked messy to me so I couldn't figure out what Aunt Esther wanted to do in there with my mother. Maybe she just wanted to make an excuse to be with Nana's things. I could understand that.

Smith and Wesson stopped by to show me their new fancy, black and blue, super awesome bicycles. They had put cards in the spokes to make the bikes sound like they had motors.

"Howdy Grace! Like our new rides?" Smith asked.

"Wow!" I was impressed. "Where did you get those bikes?"

"You mean Luke and Han?" Wesson said.

"Huh?" I looked around for some guys but didn't see anyone other than the twins.

"This here is Luke Skywalker," Wesson said introducing me to his bike.

"And this is Han Solo," Smith said pulling his bike next to me. I held my hands out and gave the handlebars a tap instead of a shake.

"Nice to meet you Luke and Hans," I said.

"It's Han, not Hans," Smith corrected.

"Oh sorry, Han," I gestured my apologies to the bike. "Those are some nice, new bikes!" I congratulated them.

"Here, take 'em for a spin!" Wesson let me take Luke for a spin, and boy did it sound mean and meaty.

After I finished, I ran to the red barn and pulled out my hot pink banana-seat bike with a white woven basket, glittery streamers, and pink ribbons. At first they laughed at my bike's dainty identity. It was very girlie, and I didn't know that streamers and ribbons were not cool or *bad to the bone*—they had informed me that's how their bikes were to be described (bad to the bone).

"Well, if we take off those ribbons and maybe spray paint the basket, it might look less, you know …"

"Less what?" I asked.

"Less lame."

Poop …

I did not want to own a lame bike so we decided to modify my bike to be cool like theirs. We spent the morning working on beefing up my dainty two-wheeler.

It still had the same spunk, but it was enhanced with a purple basket, black streamers, and a striped frame. When we were finished, Smith and Wesson were impressed.

"Last little detail we need is a card in the spokes so it can sound as good as she looks," Smith said, admiring my bike.

I ran inside but couldn't find a playing card that I was allowed to use. As I was digging in the junk drawer, I found some plastic utensils and a wild idea entered my brain.

I used an old plastic fork instead of a card in my spokes, and it made an even louder sound. When my spunky bike zoomed around with its guttural groan, I felt pretty proud of myself.

"What should we call her?" I asked. I had never thought to name my bike before like Smith and Wesson had. But after doing so much work, she deserved a name.

We all thought for a while and threw around some possibilities, "How about Karen, Dora, Geraldine?"

"Nah."

"Lucy? Lois?"

None of them went well with my bike's new awesomeness. Then the boys at the same time called out, "Princess Leia!"

AND THE PURPLE PUDDLE

⚬⚭ *Fourteen* ⚭⚬
Life in a Log

Later on in the afternoon, after the boys left, I was proudly sitting on my *bad to the bone* bike, also known as Leia, near the puddle that was getting shallower each day. It hadn't rained in a while. Mazie showed up even though it was harder to see her. I told her all about Princess Leia's new awesome sound. Instead of just telling her, I decided to show her, to better demonstrate all of our hard work.

As I was riding noisily around, a big lavender car crunched onto the gravel driveway. Who was here? I expected Aunt Esther, but she drove a white Jeep.

A fluffy-headed shadow was moving around in the front seat then out popped Mrs. Dottie Doohinkley, the saleslady from Nana's church. I could smell her putrid powdery perfume all the way over here. She was carrying a big heavy-looking satchel. Momma, who was picking weeds in the garden, looked up then hid behind the corn stalks.

Mrs. Doohinkley walked to the front porch and knocked on the Dutch door. The top half was open so she called out my momma's name.

"Oh Ruth! Ruth dear! Anyone home? It's me, Dottie Doohinkley!" She looked around hoping to find one of us.

My momma stayed quiet and crouched behind the tall green stalks. I stayed quiet too, hoping to go unnoticed by the brown-toothed lady.

"Hello! Lumen? Lu—men? Ruth? Freckle Face Grace? Are there any Newtons home?" She knocked some more.

Did she just say Freckle Face Grace?

Hope was the only one inside our home. She was studying, of course. She did a lot of that. Hope came to the door when she realized no one else would answer the nonstop calls from Mrs. Doohinkley.

"Well, hello Hope! Don't you look beautiful. I must say, you might have the world's loveliest hair. I bet you would like to have the world's loveliest skin too, wouldn't you?"

Hope backed up and seemed to wave away some of Mrs. Doohinkley's awful perfume. She looked behind Mrs. Doohinkley and spotted Momma hiding in the garden. Momma waved her hands around then put her finger up to her lips signaling Hope to keep quiet. Hope obediently pretended to be all alone.

"Aren't you going to invite me in?" Mrs. Doohinkley asked as she was poised to enter.

"Oh, um … Momma and Papa aren't home and …" Hope looked unsure.

Mrs. Doohinkley interrupted her and said, "I came all this way, I guess I can wait a little while for your mother to return. Plus, I am just parched. Would you offer me a glass of lemonade, dear? I am simply withered in this summertime heat!"

Hope opened the door for Mrs. Doohinkley then they disappeared inside. I felt sorry for Hope who was forced to entertain and oblige the pushy, smelly Dottie Doohinkley— otherwise known as Dootie Doo*stinkly*.

I heard another car coming into the driveway. This was a busy day! We rarely had visitors and to have two in one day, back to back, was certainly out of the ordinary. I almost had no time to talk to Mazie. This time it was Aunt Esther's Jeep rolling in. Before it could get too close, Momma jumped out of the garden and climbed into the open passenger seat. I hadn't seen my momma move so quickly—not since she had seen a snake crawling through her garden going after a baby bunny rabbit. Momma fought that snake off and thumped it to death. We had lots of bunny rabbits at our farm and, even though they got in the garden, they only ate their fair share. Plus, Momma had a soft spot for bunnies.

Aunt Esther's Jeep turned around in the driveway then headed back out. I told Mazie that I'd be right back. I knew where they were headed so I followed after them on foot.

This was going to be fun. I snuck around, trying to go unnoticed like a spy. I tiptoed through the thicket of woods and leaped over the bigger rocks across the silver stream that ran down the side of our super long driveway. I climbed over an old stone wall that must have been built by settlers, ages ago. It was so old-looking and crafted in such a way that told stories from another, ancient time.

The woods were filled with birds and insects all whistling and chirping to one another. I wished I understood bird calls. It would be so neat to know what they were saying.

I skipped over the old rotten fallen logs and peeked inside the hollow ends to see if there were any toads. Nope, there were only a few worms blindly scooting around. I heard my momma and aunt talking in the distance and remembered to get back on track. As I was hustling though the trail, an invisible silky web wrapped itself around my face.

Eeeeeeek!!!!

I spat and sputtered as I tried to wipe it

away. It didn't want to go so easily. I imagined a huge spiny black spider crawling all over my back as shivers quaked through my body. I jerked and ran for Nana's cabin.

I guess all my squealing didn't help me go unnoticed ... like a spy. I ran straight for Momma and shrieked that I had spiders crawling all over me.

"No, Poodle Poo, you don't have any spiders on you," she said as she spun me around and did a thorough examination. "Were you in the woods?"

"Uh-huh," I said with my face dotted in sweat.

"What were you doing in there?"

"Coming down here."

"What are you doing down here?" she asked.

"Getting away from Mrs. Doohinkley. She wants to burn away all of my freckles!" I frantically said. "Nana said they were good ... that they were angel kisses. Why would Mrs. Doohinkley call them wretched or want them gone?"

"Oh, Grace," Momma grabbed me

and gave me a hug. "No one, not even Mrs. Doohinkley's potions will ever be able to remove your beautiful freckles! They are just like Nana said, angel kisses, and I won't allow a soul to try to ever diminish a single one, okay?" Momma said as she wiped away my worry. "Now come inside with me and Aunt Esther. We are going to wait here until that Mrs. Doo*stinkly* gets the hint to scram."

I smiled because this was the first time since Nana had died that Momma had called me Poodle Poo, my pet name, and really looked into my eyes. I giggled because she called that lady Mrs. Doo*stinkly*.

I loved Momma, but, recently, she was unusually busy with cleaning, gardening, pickling, jarring, and laundry. I didn't want to get in her way. I just helped here and there to be near her, but Momma was always too preoccupied with the conversations inside her own head to talk to me or anyone else. When I did get her undivided attention, it meant a lot.

We three walked inside the cabin. It was dark and a tad dreary without my nana to warm and brighten it. My nana glowed like a pixie, especially her wide, white smile. Even though her teeth were crooked, they were friendly. I turned on the kitchen lights.

"How ya doing, hun?" Aunt Esther said to me as she gently put her hand on my shoulder.

I turned to see my aunt's warm hazel eyes that looked a little sad, I guess like mine. Aunt Esther was shorter and sturdier than Momma but her rounded face reminded me so much of Nana's. She had never married. She didn't need a man to complete her, she had said. Ol' Tex was all she needed. Ol' Tex was Aunt Esther's RV. She told us many stories about how Ol' Tex never let her down even in the most dangerous situations.

Aunt Esther traveled around the country in an RV with her best friend and traveling partner, Alice. They'd been to every state in the U.S. and even some countries south of Mexico.

"Here, honey, I brought this back from the Mayan ruins for you." Aunt Esther handed me a necklace with a big black sun charm.

"It was carved from a coconut shell. I bought it from the artist who made it. His name was Macho, and he was set up in a little grass-roofed shack."

I looked down at the necklace. The sun had a smiley face and wavy spirals around it. Turning the charm over, I noticed that it was indeed carved from a coconut shell. I pulled it over my head and let it rest around my neck. I sure was proud to have such a treasure all the way from the Mayan ruins.

"Did you say *thank you* to Aunt Esther?" Momma reminded me.

"Oh, sorry. Thank you, Aunt Esther. I love it!" I grinned. She could tell I appreciated her gift.

"Now, what is it you wanted to do in here so badly?" Momma asked Aunt Esther.

"It's not so much that I *want* to do anything in here. It's just that I knew you had a lot on your plate, and I wanted to help you if you wanted me to."

I looked around the cabin while they continued their conversation. In the living room, the great stone fireplace took up one whole wall. It was made from the grey rocks which bedded the bottom of the stream that trickled down the mountain.

Tons of family pictures were placed on

the mantle, bookshelves, and side tables. My favorite photo was one of Nana and Pop Pop on their wedding day. They looked so young and happy. They were standing on the stone steps of their parish with the tall white steeple. Nana's veil and dress blew in the wind. Pop Pop was hugging her waist laying a kiss on her that sent her backwards. He must have been very strong because even though they were on steps, his grip kept her from falling.

A picture of Momma and Papa on their wedding day was on top of the upright piano in the corner. Momma had a smirk while Papa had his thumb up, like he was the luckiest man alive to marry such a stunning, chestnut-haired beauty.

Momma was elegant. She still was, but something always seemed to bother her, and that bothered me.

I heard Momma say something to Aunt Esther that had me concerned. "Why must you always be traveling? You couldn't even come to your own mother's funeral?"

"I was in a third-world country. They don't exactly have the best phone access."

"That's what I mean. *I* couldn't even call you. I had no way of talking to my only sister to tell her that *our* mother had died. You were too busy galavanting around the world to pay any attention to our mother's needs. And now that she's gone, you want to help me? Don't you think it's a little late for that?"

Aunt Esther was quiet.

"I mean, what did you expect? She was dying for years, and you never seemed to care enough to be here for her then. Why wait until it's too late to help?"

Aunt Esther spoke. "Of course, she was dying. We *are all* dying, but I am trying to live. Momma told me to go. She told me to live while I still could which is a lot more than I can say about you. It's like the second you found out that she had cancer, you were on the same sort of self-doomed death sentence along with her." Aunt Esther shook her head. "I lost you years ago … everyone else did as well. You've been so preoccupied with being angry with me that you forgot that you had a life, too."

Cancer? Nana had cancer? I never knew she had cancer. What even was cancer? A million thoughts ran through my brain.

"Somebody had to care. Somebody had to be responsible. Somebody had to be here. But because you were so obviously going to be gone, I guess *that* responsibility was mine. So thank you for that. At least *I* won't have regrets."

"You think I have regrets? The only regret I have is the time I spent *not* living—not doing something. After talking with Mom, I made a decision to stop living for other people when I saw where that got me … nowhere. Now I don't … I mean cannot … live for anyone but myself. You have to do the same, Ruth."

"Don't tell me how to live."

"Okay, if you don't want me to tell you how to live, don't make me feel guilty for living the way that I do."

I'd had enough of their quarrels. I walked up the carpeted stairs and went into Nana's bedroom. I walked around and sat in front of Nana's vanity.

I had watched her putting on her makeup many times before her dances. She'd poof some powder on her nose and cheeks then take her red lipstick and twirl it around her lips before she'd make a pucker and pop them. At the end of her routine, she'd draw a mole on the side of her mouth and call it a beauty mark.

One evening, Nana made a big fuss getting me all ready to go to the dance with her. She'd made a special dress that had layers and layers of colorful ruffles. She had carefully wrapped my wild, straggly hair around banana clips. While we were waiting for my hair to set she gave me a beauty mark in the same spot as she had placed hers. I found her fake eyelashes and held them up to my eyelids pretending to be glamourous. As I looked in the mirror, I could see the whole scene from that night. That was a great night.

I walked over to the edge of Nana's bed then lay back on the quilts. Nana had made hundreds of beautiful quilts. We each had one specially made for us on our first birthdays. So as not to take any chances, she wouldn't start them until the day we were born. Nana came from a time when having babies was dangerous not just for the baby but also for the momma. It was considered bad luck to make certain heirlooms for unborn children according to her belief. Plus, she had to see if it was a boy or a girl and what our names would be so she could have it embroidered.

Her bedroom had a warm-red feeling even though the walls were wooden, like the outside of her cottage. It was a log cabin in a sense, but it didn't have round logs—they were square with hard, white, frosting-looking stuff in between the stacked wood.

The bed covers were so comfy; the pillows reminded me of Nana when she had hugged me last. I must have gotten a little too comfortable because I heard my name being called while my eyes had been shut and my body was sleeping.

"There you are." Momma came in and sat on the bed.

I yawned as I slowly sat up. "Why are you guys fighting?" I asked as I rubbed my eyes.

"Oh." She looked embarrassed. "That's just what sisters do sometimes, I guess."

Hope and I didn't fight that much, but we weren't grown up like Momma and Aunt Esther. Maybe sisters fought more when they grew up. I hoped to not get older just so I wouldn't have to fight with Hope because I liked Hope.

"What's cancer?" I asked. Momma breathed out and with her breath came tears. Momma cried. I guess cancer is bad because simply saying the word made Momma weep.

Aunt Esther came into the bedroom and sat on the bed, wrapped her arms around Momma, and cried too. She must have been standing outside the door listening to our conversation. Aunt Esther looked over to me, with one of her arms she took my hand and gently squeezed it as we all cried. I wasn't sure why I was crying, but seeing them cry made me tear up.

After some time, Momma spoke. "By the way, Esther, I wasn't mad at you. I was mad at cancer. I guess I just took out all of my frustration on you. I'm sorry."

Aunt Esther looked over at her and tearfully smiled. "That's okay, you're right, I should have been here with all of you."

They gave each other another long, necessary hug.

"Well, we'll be here all night if we don't get going," Momma said after the tear storm cleared.

"Yes, let's start clearing things out," Aunt Esther agreed. They emptied out Nana's closet of all her beautiful dresses and blouses and dungarees (that's what Nana called jeans). Eventually, a pile of garments filled a couple of boxes.

"What are you going to do with all her clothes?" I asked.

"We're donating them to The Salvation Army," Aunt Esther said.

"Oh." For some reason I had trouble knowing that when they hauled all of Nana's clothes away, I'd never be able to smell them again. I held one of her favorite sweaters up to my nose. It smelled like dryer sheets and cookies—like Nana. I didn't want to lose her scent but when I went to say something, I saw Momma and Aunt Esther sharing a peaceful moment as they tried on some of Nana's jewelry.

"Esther, you must take this, she got that from her mother, Grandma Markarian," Momma said.

"No, you're the one with daughters to pass this on to. It has to stay in the family."

"My daughters *are* your daughters. You can

always give whatever you want to them."

Aunt Esther looked over at me and tightened her lips. She must have been feeling an extra tender emotion.

"Thank you, Ruth. That means a lot." She sniffed then said, "Since I apparently already gave you my same hair color, Grace, come see what's yours when *I* die."

Aunt Esther and I had matching strawberry-blonde locks, only hers were cut in layers up to her shoulders. I walked over to see a beautiful fiery stone set in a silver-colored band. "What is it?" I asked.

"It's an opal set in platinum. Only people born in October are allowed to wear them. And since you, Nana, and I are all October babies … well, you get the gist."

"It's *so* beautiful. It's white but it looks like it's on fire inside," I marveled.

"Look, when you turn it, it turns blue," Momma said.

"Wow!" It turned blue all right and even pink, orange, plus some other in-between shades.

&‑ • ‑&

The day that turned into late afternoon and Aunt Esther's Jeep was loaded with piles of Nana's special clothes.

I saw headlights coming down the hill as a big lavender car pulled up to the cabin—out popped Dottie Doohinkley like a terrifying jack-in-the-box.

"That woman has a lot of nerve," Momma said under her breath.

"Ruth!" Mrs. Doohinkley exclaimed. "Oh, I'm so glad I caught you! I've been waiting for hours. Hope was kind enough to invite me in. I gave her a makeover ... *on the house* ... this time," she proudly broadcasted. She held up the backside of her palm to her mouth and quietly said, "You can pay me back later with a small favor," she had whispered as if it was a treat. "But actually, I really wanted to talk to you ... Oh! Who's this?"

She was asking about Aunt Esther. Excitement filled her face when she realized that she might have more than one customer. She glanced over Aunt Esther's unfussy appearance then said, "You could use some of these amazing products. You look like you've been neglecting your skin, dear. Come on over here." She signaled for Aunt Esther to get examined more thoroughly. Her eyes looked like they turned into laser beams scanning Aunt Esther's face and hands.

"*Hmmmmmmm*. How old are you?"

Aunt Esther looked a little worried but obliged the pushy lady. "I'm thirty-nine."

Mrs. Doohinkley got close to Aunt Esther's face and said, "You don't exfoliate do you?"

Mrs. Doohinkley turned to Momma and I as if we were her personal audience. "I cannot stress how important it is to exfoliate your skin! I mean look at me … I'm fifty-five years old, and I'm told almost daily that I don't look a day over thirty-five!" Her purple hair bounced as she proudly emphasized her delusional statement. "I'll tell you … just the other day, some young man said I looked younger than thirty! Can you imagine?" Her mouth stood wide, smiling with pride.

"No," I said, because she definitely looked fifty-five if not sixty to me.

She threw her unsmiling stare in my direction.

"Don't be rude, dear," Mrs. Doohinkley said. "Ruth, you really should discipline her more, otherwise you are going to have a big problem on your hands." She pointed her long fingernails at me. "I mean look at those tattered clothes, and, tell me, why does she have those wings on her back? It's high time you did something about that and those awful freckles of hers."

"Being honest is *not* rude," Momma said. "What *is* rude, is *you* bombarding me and my family with trying to sell us worthless products. I am not interested in Cary Mae, ways of getting a down payment on a purple *old* lady car, getting rid of Grace's beautiful freckles, or a hideous clown-faced makeover. Now, please leave!"

Mrs. Doohinkley was stunned into silence. I'm not sure if Mrs. Doohinkley had ever been silent in her life. I don't think she knew how to be quiet or what to do while so. A twitch came over her left cheek; she placed her palm on her face to calm it. She felt her skin, perhaps to see if it was still slathered in makeup, then slowly lowered herself back into the driver's side of her big lavender car and away she drove.

⚘ *Fifteen* ⚘

The Chestnut Tree

I had a little too much fun recounting the story about Mrs. Doohinkley to Mazie in the puddle.

"Ha ha ha!" she giggled. "That's funny! I'm glad your mother wasn't too afraid to tell her off."

"Me, too."

"So what's going to happen with all of

Nana's clothes?" Mazie seemed concerned.

"I guess they are all going to be taken to The Salvation Army." I didn't like the sound of that.

"Don't you want to keep any?"

"Of course, I do, but I'm not sure that I will fit into any of them."

"But what if you made something that you *could* wear out of them?" Mazie suggested.

"Like what?"

A pebble plopped into the puddle, and Mazie disappeared.

"Hey! Where'd that come from?" I looked up and saw Abel ready to throw another pebble. I knew what he wanted so I got to my feet and chased him up a tree. Wrapped in his cape, he scrambled and scooted up a tall chestnut tree giggling all the way. When he got to his favorite branch, he wrapped his legs around it and hung upside down like an opossum. I hung upside down next to him. The dusky world looked different from this perspective. It felt good to let my head dangle. With all the blood rushing to my head, my eyes felt like they were bulging.

"Where's Nana?" Abel asked in his scratchy voice.

I wasn't sure that I was qualified to answer such a question, but as his older sister of two years, I knew it was my obligation. I turned right-side up to have this serious conversation. He also turned right-side up, and now our legs dangled from the limb.

His big brown eyes looked like shiny chocolate chips as they searched my face for answers. He scratched one of his dirty, chubby cheeks waiting for me to talk.

I took a deep breath then went for it. "Well, apparently, they were running low on kissing angels." Abel looked confused at first so I explained myself. "Those are the angels who kiss little kids with everlasting lipstick while they're sleeping so when the kids wake up, freckles are left behind—also known as angel lipstick … it never comes off," I explained in all sincerity. "Anyway, they must have been running low on kissing angels because I had barely gotten any freckles in a while, but the other night I was having a dream that Nana was kissing me, and when I woke up in the morning, I had a new freckle! See here?" I pointed to my nose and said, "That's a new freckle! I now have seventeen freckles in all, and I think it's from Nana."

Abel's eyes grew with the thought of Nana's nighttime kisses.

"Oh! And would you lookie here! I think Nana must have kissed you, too. You have a new freckle right there." I pointed to his sweaty little chin. He put his finger on it to make sure he wouldn't lose it then scuttled down the tree one-handed. He ran into the house, accidentally slamming the screen door. I ran after him, accidentally slamming the screen door, too.

"Stop slamming the doors!" Momma called out.

"Sorry!" I said while smelling the hovering stench of Dottie Doostinkley's perfume.

I pounded the planks as I climbed upstairs. Abel was found on top of his step stool gawking in the mirror. He had his finger pointing to his freckle with a smile on his face.

"I see it!" he said excitedly.

"See what?" Hope asked, her face caked with the makeup that Mrs. Doohinkley had smothered onto it.

"Nana's kiss," Abel explained.

Hope looked confused. "Huh? Where?" she asked.

"Right here, on my chin!"

Hope leaned in to investigate. "That's just a freckle, Abel."

"Nuh-uh! Grace said that Nana is a kissing angel now, and she wears lipstick that leaves a mark that never comes off."

Hope looked at me like I was loonies. "Where do you come up with this stuff? I mean, it is clever, but really ... we all know that when you die, you don't turn into some mythical creature or go to some fictional place."

"How do you know?" I asked.

Hope rolled her eyes as if I asked the dumbest question. But since she was my smarter, older sister, she explained herself. "According to my scientific studies, there is no evidence of an afterlife. When you die, it's over. You just decompose like everything else."

Abel and I didn't like the sound of that. I guess she could see it on our down-turned faces. "Don't be so sad!" she tried to console us. "It's just part of life."

"But, how do you know?" I asked again.

"Have you died before?"

She seemed a tad amused by my question like she was ready to explain away all my thoughts.

"Science."

I didn't know how one single word in particular could prove me wrong so I said. "How?"

"Really, Grace you should read more books. Books on physics, biology, and evolution."

I loved looking at books with fanciful pictures, but when it came down to reading the words, all the letters would dance around on the page, not allowing me to read them.

"If those books make it so I won't believe in angels and an afterlife, why would I *want* to read them? If I wanted to read a book, I would want to read books that give me hope for something when we die, not books that give me nothing."

"The reality is, there is nothing," Hope began.

"So why is everything only here? Only when we're alive?"

"What do you mean?"

"Why would everything only exist here or now? Why couldn't something exist after we die? Has anyone ever died before and come back?"

"Yes, I think so," Hope hesitantly answered.

"What did those people say?"

"Some people say that they saw a bright light, but that could be explained by brain waves short circuiting."

"Well, when I look up into the starry sky at night, I know that there is more out there than I can see. I know that things exist in the great beyond."

"That's because scientists and astronomers have gone and explored those places."

I thought for a little bit about the thoughts that were spinning around in my head while trying to make some sense of what Hope was saying and what I was thinking. They were so different.

"So, scientists have been every-single-where and have seen every-single-thing? They know everything there is to know?" I asked.

"Well, no. Not exactly."

"So there's a chance that they might not

know everything? And there could be *something* in the afterlife?"

"Yes, I guess so," she reluctantly agreed.

"Maybe it's, you believe whatever you *want* to believe," I said, then asked, "Do you believe you're going to be a record-breaking astronaut?"

I knew Hope believed that one day with lots and lots of hard work, she would achieve her dream so I knew she wouldn't just brush off my question.

"Yes."

"Because you believe it! I believe that there is something more to this life, something bigger than all of us and this whole world."

"How do you know?" She turned the same line of questioning on me.

"Because otherwise there is no reason for anything … living or dying, wanting to do anything, to have thoughts, feelings, happiness, prettiness, or sadness … love or life."

She laughed off my conclusion. "You can believe what you want to believe, but until I see otherwise, I'll trust my science books." Her tone of voice sounded aloof.

Why did Hope sound so *hopeless*? "You

don't have to *not* believe just because all the science books tell you to believe in nothing. You *can* think for yourself," I said.

Hope sort of smiled then said, "Until I see otherwise, I'll trust my science books," as she started back to her room.

I shrugged. "What about dang gravity?"

"Huh?" She turned back around.

"I mean just gravity."

"What about it?"

"Just because you can't see it doesn't mean that it doesn't exist."

Hope looked stumped for an instant. "Whatever." She turned back and walked into her room.

Abel looked back into the mirror at his freckle and asked, "So, is it a Nana kiss or not?"

I re-inspected his freckle closely. He held still so I could get a good look. It was in a sloppy shape of a heart! I knew for sure now. "It's definitely an angel kiss from Nana, Abel! Look, it's a heart!"

❧ *Sixteen* ❧

Lightbulb

As I was about to drift off to sleep, an idea of what I could do with Nana's clothes woke me, which made me go downstairs to get them from Aunt Esther's Jeep. I put what I could carry in a pile inside my closet. After I gathered all that I could, I arranged them in my thoughts, knowing exactly what I could do with them.

In the morning, Abel and I took the

clothes back to Nana's cottage. I hid them in the sewing room in piles just like all the other piles of scraps she had organized.

"What are you going to do with all of this?" Abel asked.

"It's a surprise." I said with big bulging eyes. Abel looked excited to be part of a surprise. "Do you want to help me?"

"Yeah!" he clapped his hands and giggled the way he did when he liked something.

"Okay, I'm going to cut up these pieces, then I need you to lay them flat to be ironed," I explained in the same tone Nana used when she would instruct me. I put on some of Nana's sewing music to get the mood just right.

We worked for hours and Abel never once complained. Instead, he sang along with me and the music.

After we finished cutting all the shapes and ironed all the pieces, we took a supper break. Boy, were we hungry. Abel was getting washed up for supper while I told Mazie all about my day. I noticed that the puddle was getting even more shallow; I could almost see the bottom.

"That's a great idea," Mazie said but with

a little less umph (that's what Nana called excitement) than normal.

"I thought you'd like that idea."

"I can't think of anything that would be better. Make sure you show me when you're finished."

"Okay, I promise!"

I started to ask Mazie one last question, but I heard the screen door slam and Momma called out to stop slamming the door before she yelled for me, "Grace! I need you to come in here and help with supper."

"Coming, Momma!"

After we set the table and gathered everyone around, I asked if we could say grace. It was something Nana always did before she ate. Since she wasn't around to do it anymore, I decided it was now my job to take over.

Papa and Momma shared a smirk then said, "Sure."

I closed my eyes as the same words Nana had repeated over and over were said, not realizing that I had memorized them.

"Thank you, Grace," Momma said.

"You're welcome." I looked over to Hope

just as she was rolling her eyes.

"You know, for the life me, I can't figure out what happened to all those clothes!" Momma said as she was passing around the biscuits. Abel and I stole glances at one another. I gave him a silent shush.

"I've been seeing Noodle wearing some clothes, maybe that's what happened," Papa guessed.

"Noodle took my mother's clothes?" Momma asked skeptically.

Papa shrugged and said, "Strange things have happened."

Aunt Esther stole a glance at Abel and me. Her right eyebrow lifted in a knowing manner, but when my scared face made a connection to hers, she winked, assuring me that my secret was safe with her. What a relief!

"So what were you and Abel doing all day?" Papa asked.

"It's a surprise," Abel blurted with a mouthful of potatoes.

"Abel!" Momma gasped. "You're eating real food! Honey Bear, I'm so proud of you! What a big boy you are!"

Abel stuffed some yellow squash in his mouth as we all cheered! He giggled. He liked getting everyone excited about his eating.

"You must have worked up quite an appetite," Papa snickered.

"Yup!" he muffled with food in his chubby cheeks.

"Hey, Abel, if you and Grace keep this up …" Papa pointed to Abel's mouth with his fork, "You can take him any day to do whatever your surprise is."

That made us both very happy. We grinned at each other with both of our mouths stuffed with food. Hope rolled her eyes again.

❧ *Seventeen* ❧

The Wrong Side of the Bed

I must have woken up on the wrong side of the bed, at least that's what Momma said after I had made a mess of everything one morning. I had finished eating my chopped up hard-boiled egg and buttered toast which normally made me full and happy. But something didn't feel right, and I guess I wasn't my usual happy self.

I thought about going back upstairs to

my bedroom, falling back to sleep, and then waking up on the right side of the bed so that maybe my mood might improve.

Abel had run through the kitchen, accidentally bonking me on the head.

On any other day, I would have just said *ow* and rubbed my head until it felt better. Instead, I yelled loudly and said mean words that I am too ashamed to repeat.

I must have looked like a dragon burning down a castle. Everyone looked at me like they were shocked and a tiny bit scared. I knew I had over-reacted, but I just couldn't help it. It just came out.

"Grace! You need to apologize to Abel for yelling at him," Momma said.

"I don't need to 'pologize! He's the one who hit me! He's the little skunk who started it!"

Abel looked hurt by my insult. And for a second, I regretted being so mean.

"Now, that is not how we talk to one another in this house!" Momma said with a lot more anger in her voice.

"Fine then, I'll just get out of this house," I said as I stood up and ran outside slamming the screen door behind me.

"Don't you slam that door!" Momma called as I ran. "Grace, you get yourself a switch and bring it back here! It's time to tan that back-talking little hide of yours!"

I knew I should have gone back upstairs to my bedroom and fallen back asleep so that I could have avoided all this. Now I was in a real pickle. I couldn't go inside, or I'd get a spanking, but if I stayed out here too long, that spanking would get worse for me the longer I delayed.

I wasn't sure what to do. If only I could go back in time, I would never have been so mean to Abel. His eyes had immediately filled with tears when I had yelled at him. I knew he never meant to hit me in the head. I was just being too sensitive. I wished Nana were home so I could run to her house to tell her about what happened and ask her what I should do … but she was gone.

I thought of the next best friend I had. I ran toward my purple puddle so I could talk to Mazie. She always helped, plus I could feel Nana's presence while I visited with her. As I got closer, I could tell something was wrong. I found the twinkling tree but there was no puddle. What happened to Mazie?

I saw the dried up spot where the puddle once had been. It was all cracked like a muddy broken mirror. Where was Mazie? Was she stuck under the mud? Was she suffocating? Would I ever see her again?? I began to panic. Without Mazie, I was nothing! Where was she?

Tears streamed down my cheeks. I threw myself at the base of the tree bawling for what seemed like forever.

I heard someone walking toward me. I thought it might be Momma ready to give me my whipping, but, instead, I heard Hope ask, "What's the matter with you?"

Without caring how silly it would sound, I told her, "My puddle is gone! I'll never see her again! My pretty purple puddle is gone!"

Hope was silent for a second, probably trying to figure out if I was crazy. "You're kidding me, right? Are you really upset about a stupid mud puddle?"

"Mazie's not some stupid mud puddle!" I yelled back.

Hope was quiet for a minute, but my head was turned away so I couldn't read her expression. "Mazie? Who … I mean what are you talking about, Grace? You sound ridiculous."

I tried to think of a way to explain Mazie to Hope, but the right words weren't coming to me. "*You* wouldn't understand." I sniffed.

"You're right. I truly can't understand why you would be more upset about a puddle than you were about Nana's death. You hardly shed one tear!" She paused. "I *don't* get it. *You* are absolutely right." The disappointment that went along with her words stung.

I had no words for a reply because what she said held some truth. I looked at her with my eyes still blurry from all my tears. Hope shook her head and walked away. I saw Momma and Papa holding Abel's hands as they witnessed our discussion. Abel looked like he was hurt but not by me yelling at him, more by seeing me so upset. I felt strangely confused.

Momma walked over. Instead of whipping me, she hugged me. I grabbed onto her gut and burst into tears. "Oh, honey, I get it. It's okay to be upset. It's okay to cry. Let it all out!"

The temporary holding back of tears was released. I pictured Nana's face over and over and how I would never see it again or touch her soft fuzzy skin. I'd never hear her sing or tell me silly stories about her and Pop Pop. It hurt so bad to feel the broken part of my heart.

I had avoided it before, somehow. Maybe always having Mazie to talk to made it so I couldn't feel the sadness I was meant to feel earlier.

Papa and Abel came over, and we all hugged until Momma said, "C'mon, Poodle Poo, let's go up to bed."

I sniffed while wiping away my snuggies and tears. "But it's still morning," Abel said, fearing the dreaded bedtime.

"Don't worry, *you* don't have to go to beddy-bye," Momma assured him as we walked inside the house.

Momma and I went upstairs. She lay with me on the bed while I hiccupped and let my tears dry. She didn't say much. She was just with me.

I must have fallen asleep by accident, but this time, I woke up on the right side of the bed.

I was awakened by her talking with Hope. I overheard Momma say, "No, dear, of course she wasn't really crying over a puddle. Sometimes young children don't react to death the way adults do. They might not act the way you'd think. Kids cry in movies because they're actors but real children grieve in a spectrum of ways. Sometimes it comes out over trivial matters. Like this situation—a puddle. All the little things that happened today gave Grace the ability to truly grieve over Nana. You see, she *was* crying about Nana, not a puddle."

But I was crying about Mazie, too, I thought to myself. Mazie was my link to Nana, and now I had lost them both ... that was just too much for me.

ᥬ *Eighteen* ᥬ

Mashed Potato Castle
Sir Broccolot
Lord Spudrick
Lady Gwenogravy

Dinner was quieter than normal, even though it was delicious. A hunk of pot roast, broccoli trees, and yummy mashed potatoes filled my flowery plate. The gravy was extra savory, and it comforted my belly like a warm Nana hug.

Aunt Esther dropped a couple of biscuit

crumbs on the floor which Noodle ran over and picked up.

I looked over at Hope who was gently feeding herself. Abel was making his mashed potatoes into what looked like a castle with gravy around it like a moat.

Most of the time, Abel's food was used for anything but his own nourishment. I watched as he carefully used a chunk of meat for a drawbridge after he set up pieces of broccoli around his castle like a forest.

"Is that Sir Broccolot galloping over to Castle Spudragon looking for Lady Gwenogravy?" Papa asked with a smile on top of his bulging cheeks. Abel half shrugged and then played along. I giggled when he picked up a small piece of biscuit and pretended to be galloping toward the mashed potato castle. He looked at me, smiled, then giggled too.

"King Biscuit of the round rolling pin," Abel snickered as he spoke in an ancient manner.

"I'm sorry for yelling at you, Abel. I know you didn't mean to hit me," I said.

In his scratchy voice, Abel said, "It's okay, Grace." Then he popped a big piece of broccoli into his gallant happy mouth.

We were all surprised as Abel chewed and swallowed the rest of his dinner without a fuss.

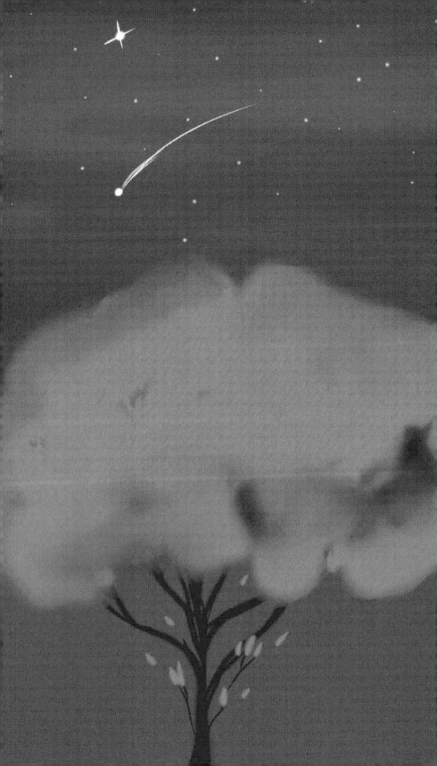

❧ Nineteen ☙

Shooting Star

With my hands holding my chin, I gazed outside of my opened bedroom window hoping to spot a shooting star that I could wish upon. The sky was the blackest blue imaginable with dots twinkling to the rhythm of a hushed harmony. Off in the distance, I heard an owl hooting.

I wiggled one of my loose teeth around with

my tongue. I felt the pit of raw gum beneath the sharp tooth roots. I wiggled my bottom tooth around harder to see if I could pull it out, but I was too scared to yank on it before it was ready. It was *so* close to coming out.

I imagined the Tooth Fairy floating around my room searching for my tooth under my pillow and not finding one. Boy, could I use some money from the Tooth Fairy about now. That money would go toward the surprise I had been planning. My eyelids fluttered and then …

Zoom!

A shooting star streaked across the sky! Papa had told me that if I saw a shooting star, I should make a wish. I was lucky to have seen it when I did because my eyes were just about to close. I shot up like a rake in the grass, smashing someone in the face. I saw that happen to Mr. Springfield, Smith and Wesson's daddy, one time, and it made us all laugh hysterically. He, however, got knocked silly.

Okay, I needed to concentrate. I had to think hard before I made my wish. It was crucial that I wished correctly. I didn't want to ruin this, possibly once in a lifetime, opportunity.

I closed my eyes, whispered my wish, and hoped with all my heart that it would come true.

I slept with a smile that night and woke extra early to rain coming down like a waterfall. I closed the window. A hurricane must have been coming through. I looked outside my bedroom window to see the wind twisting, bending trees around in positions they were never intended to lean.

Abel came into my room with sleep still covering his features. He had on his cape as usual but also had his giant stuffed-horse named Milkshake.

"Hey there, Buckaroo, what's Milkshake doing out of his corral?" Hope asked. I hadn't seen her standing in the doorframe of my room until now.

"He's headed out to burn the breeze, go on an adventure … lookin' for new pasture to graze," Abel said as if he really knew Milkshake's mind.

"Oh, I see," she said.

"How long has it been storming like this?" I asked Hope.

"Since 4:00 AM. I woke up from the first whistle of wind. I knew it was coming because I had heard about the forecast on the television, but all the meteorological predictions said it wouldn't come till later today. I guess it decided to come early."

"I guess you can't believe everything the experts say," I said with a little shade of sass.

"Ha ha," she said with a cynical smile. "Guess *you're* feeling better."

I smiled because I was.

"What should we do today?" Abel asked. "How are you and I going to …" I put my finger up to his mouth shushing him.

"*SHHHHH!*" I didn't want Abel to accidentally tell Hope about any of my surprises that I had in store.

"Really?" Hope said. "You're going to be that infantile? What are you guys up to? It's not like I care or anything. I'm just curious."

"What are you curious about?" I asked.

"What you're doing."

"But, how do you know we're doing something?"

"Huh?" she said, clearly confused.

I tried to be clearer, not wanting to antagonize her. "You haven't seen us doing anything, so what makes you believe that we are?"

"I know what you're trying to do here and it won't work."

I realized too what I was doing, unintentionally at first, but then decided to go with it since I was already halfway there. I casually petted Milkshake, putting on airs of ease when I said, "Okay, then just believe that we are doing nothing because you don't know or haven't seen otherwise."

Hope looked at me in her usual condescending manner. She was used to being the smartest person she knew. She was used to me being the younger, simpler sister, (and I still was), but, somehow, maybe because of all the things Nana had said to me along the way of my time with her, I knew something Hope didn't.

It didn't give me satisfaction to know more than Hope; it actually made me feel sad because I wanted Hope to feel the happiness and joy Nana had always given to me. I also knew that

Hope needed to figure things out for herself. Nobody can make anyone believe in something or anything.

"Want to help me build a blanket fort?" I asked Hope.

"Yeah!" Abel volunteered.

"I think I'll sit this one out," Hope said as she turned to leave.

"How about this?" I didn't want Hope to feel left out so I said, "We'll surprise you with the world's *BEST* blanket fort *EVER* in less than fifteen minutes!"

"We'll see about that," she doubtfully said as she went back to her sophisticated scientific room.

After she was gone, Abel and I quickly got to work. We grabbed knives and big cardboard boxes from downstairs, stacked toys upon shelves and strung lights along the edges of the room then cut out shapes in old sheets and stuck lights around in different places until it was just right.

"Hope, we're ready for you," I informed her as she was hunched over a book at her desk.

"That was way more than fifteen minutes,"

she playfully jabbed.

"Perfection is worth waiting for," I assured her.

"Perfection?" she questioned as we walked over to my room.

"I guess I'll let you be the judge of that," I burbled.

"Why, thank you, Grace." She sounded like Momma when she said that.

I opened the door to my darkened room. My ceiling light was off, and we had put an extra curtain over the window so the room was unlit. And since it was still so shadowed and somber outside, it wasn't hard to get a rich, dark ambience.

"Aren't you going to turn on the lights so I can see?"

"Hope, look for your spaceship."

"My spaceship?"

Abel switched on the flashlight that illuminated the cardboard spaceship we had constructed. "Enter in the secret code to gain access," Abel said in a robot voice.

"I don't know the secret code."

"Well, you should because it's all about

you. *You are* the secret code," I said trying to give her a clue. Little did she know, there was no code … All she had to do was pretend.

At first she didn't know what I was talking about but then got the hint, "Oh, okay." She punched in some imaginary numbers that I enhanced with *beep boop* sound effects until the door to the spaceship opened with a hiss.

We entered the inner chamber. Abel turned on a spinning colorful light that was supposed to illuminate our control center.

We pretended to get buckled in and prepared for liftoff. Abel did the countdown … "In five … four … three … two … one … liftoff!" Abel and I provided the necessary sounds for liftoff until we reached orbit.

Hope couldn't help but have fun as we floated in imaginary space. I had "stolen" a lamp of hers that projected different constellations. Hope and I were cleared for a spacewalk so we exited the vessel. Abel flicked on the other lights over the holey sheets to make it appear like we were floating in the cosmos. I looked over at Hope's face; it was exactly as I had pictured it would be, filled with wonder and joy.

"Is this where you've always wanted to go?" I asked.

"Yes!" she said.

"How did you know it existed?"

Hope was silent for a minute but then released her doubt and said, "Because I believed it did."

✂ *Twenty* ✂

Wet Jeep

The storm took three whole days to pass, leaving a mess of tree limbs and debris everywhere. Aunt Esther was stuck here until her Jeep could dry out.

"Good thing Noodle stole all those clothes, or they would have been ruined!" Aunt Esther said with a wink in my direction.

Papa chuckled.

I snorted.

Noodle clucked.

"I guess so," Momma agreed.

The blue sky was a welcomed sight after so much darkness. On sunny days like this, I couldn't wait to go outside. Papa was rushing to take Abel to a soccer training camp because Abel needed to run most days.

After breakfast, I made my plans for the day. I had a long list of responsibilities that I had created for myself. At the top of my list, was the pile of sewing that waited for me at Nana's. Looks like I was going to be sewing alone today.

"Wish me luck," I told Momma after I had packed up my pail and set off to work. I was trying to sound grownup.

"Good luck Grace, on whatever it is you're up to."

"See you later, Grace," Aunt Esther said as I accidentally slammed the screen door.

"How many times do I have to say it?" Momma exhaustedly said.

"Sorry!" I called back as I trotted along on my way.

Before I went to Nana's cabin, I looked around at the freshly washed trees and gleaming grass. Bright emerald greens and periwinkle blues intermingled along the sky's backdrop. Globes of dandelions tempted me to blow on them, scattering their seeds. Birds whistled and chirruped songs as they flickered back and forth along tree branches. Squirrels squeaked before sitting up straight to munch on acorns.

From the corner of my eye, a sparkle came from under my special twinkling tree. I squinted, looking again.

Could it be?

It was! My purple puddle! I ran over and saw Mazie, overflowing with rain water.

"Mazie! You're back!"

Mazie smiled bigger than ever.

"I thought I'd never see you again," I lamented.

"Like all living things, as long as I get plenty of water, I'll always be around."

I giggled gleefully. Seeing Mazie in the puddle looking so happy made me extra joyful. My wish had come true ... well, most of it. I wished upon that shooting star and voilà!

Maybe the rest of my wishes would come true when the time was right. I told Mazie all about the conversation I had had with Hope and that I thought about telling her about my surprise.

"Maybe you should wait and surprise her, too," Mazie suggested. "She needs to feel special."

"You're right," I agreed. "I just thought it would be nice for us to work together."

"You'll work together when the time is right," Mazie assured me as I got up to go get to work.

"You're right again," I said before Mazie disappeared.

I preferred the wooded route to Nana's cabin. It was more adventurous. I liked looking at all the different animals along the way. It wasn't that long of a hike, but for some reason I was extra hungry today.

I was glad that I had packed a pail full of leftovers from last night's supper. Even though I probably should have waited, I devoured it as soon as I got inside Nana's kitchen.

Her picture window looked over the meadow across the way to her dance barn. As

I was chewing, I had a vision of all my family dancing together—how fun it would be. I thought about the whole evening and hatched some exciting plans. If I was going to make my ideas work, I had to get going.

I worked tirelessly the rest of the afternoon to the beat of Nana's special sewing tunes. The tempo and rhythm provided just enough "umph" to keep me going. The sweet singing of old spirituals seemed to go along with each drop and stitch of the needle.

No one would have called me a gifted seamstress before, but it seemed as if some of Nana's essence or talent had transferred to me after she had died.

From downstairs, I heard the door creak open. Who was it? I heard footsteps coming up the stairs. They weren't anyone's footsteps I recognized. Nana's sewing room was in the upstairs extra bedroom; I had hoped to have stayed hidden there until my surprise was ready. I was as still as a log when Aunt Esther popped her head into the room.

"Hi Grace!"

"Oh, it's you! What a relief!"

"I'm glad you think so. I was hoping not to discourage you from whatever you're up to," she said with a smile.

"Aunt Esther, I know you'll keep my secret," I said with a big wink.

"I will definitely keep your secret because I don't know what it is," she tittered. "And by the way, Grace, you don't need to tell me what it is either. Just know that I think you're an amazing little girl."

Mazie had told me that I was amazing, too. I wondered why they thought I was *amazing*. I was pretty sure that I was ordinary like Hope and Abel, but then again, when I thought more about each of them, like how Hope was so dedicated to her future plans of being a record-breaking astronaut and how Abel could run faster and longer than most boys his age, they were pretty amazing, too. It must run in the family.

Maybe that's why Abel knew he should wear a superhero cape because superheroes were amazing. And that's why Hope was serious about her studies because record-breaking astronauts were amazing. But what was so amazing about me? I didn't wear a cape or study hard. I was just me, Grace Newton.

"How'd you like to have a little break and have some hot cocoa with me?" Aunt Esther asked.

Hot cocoa sounded delicious right about now. "Oh! I'd like that!" I said, patting my belly. I followed my aunt downstairs to the kitchen where a red kettle was already singing its steamy song. Aunt Esther put three scoops of cocoa in each mug then poured in the boiling water. She topped off the cocoa with a splash of cream and a big puffy marshmallow. She handed the steamy mug to me with a spoon to stir it. I blew on the hot drink and bravely took a sip.

"You can drink it that hot?" she asked.

"I like it hot!"

"Oh gosh, I think I'm going to have to get an ice cube, this is molten lava."

"It's called *hot* cocoa not *warm* cocoa!" I said while I spooned in another sip.

"I guess you're right about that. My traveling buddy, Alice, can drink things hot like you."

"Where's Alice, now?" I asked.

"She's visiting her folks in Tennessee but

she'll be here soon."

"Oh, I have a loose tooth," I said while wiggling it around with my finger.

"Oh, do you now? Let's have a look," Aunt Esther said while pretending to be serious, like a dentist.

She examined the inside of my mouth. "Aha! That *is* a loose tooth! That one's sure to garner a couple of quarters, in my expert opinion," she said while taking a confident sip of her cocoa.

"What's cancer?" I asked.

Aunt Esther spit out her cocoa, spewing it across the countertop which caused me to laugh. She shook her head and wiped her mouth. She stood up, grabbed a dishtowel to mopped up her mess.

"I'm glad you didn't wait until I had piping hot cocoa in my mouth to ask me that. Oh, wait … you did," she stated jovially.

I could tell she was trying to delay her response. I waited silently as she realized I wasn't going to be distracted.

"Well, Grace … cancer is … uh, cancer is an illness that causes some people to die."

"Nana died from cancer, right?"

"Yes." She sat back down on the barstool next to me.

"Can some people *not* die from cancer?"

"Well, there are ways that people can get treatment and then live longer, but as you know, everyone will die someday."

"Could Nana have gotten treatment so she could have lived longer?"

"In her case, the treatment was just as dangerous as her not getting it."

"Where do you get cancer?"

"What do you mean? It's not contagious like a cold."

"No, I mean, where do you get cancer in your body?"

"Oh, well, let's see, there's breast cancer, skin cancer, pancreatic cancer, but Nana had bone cancer. It actually started as breast cancer, and she had lots of chemotherapy treatment before you were ever born. She even had a double mastectomy and was cured for years, but it had metastasized when it returned. She said she couldn't be a guinea pig again. In fact, she never went to see another medical doctor for the rest of her life."

"The rest of her life?" I repeated in disbelief.

"She was only supposed to live for six months so at first it didn't seem like it would be very long when she had made up her mind. But she beat the odds and lived twelve more years, largely because of her diet, your parents, and you kids. Right after she wrote off the medical treatments, she came here to live—when Hope was born. Your mother named her Hope, for your nana. She hoped that just saying her name so often would actually give everyone around them the right words to heal your nana. And when you were born five years later and Nana was still alive, she knew grace had visited this family and she was thankful."

"What about Abel?"

"When he was born, your mother was in awe of all the things your Nana was able to do. You saw how she could do yard work, housework, babysit you kids, cook meals for crowds, sew garments all day long and she still had enough energy to sing and dance. And she loved to dance. Your Nana was all three: hope, grace, and able. She beat cancer two times, and the second time, she did it on her terms which turned out to be better. She never had to get any more of her body parts cut off," Aunt Esther said.

"That is better. If I ever get cancer, I'm going to do what Nana did."

"What's that?"

"Live."

"I'll drink to that! Cheers!" Aunt Esther held up her mug, and I held up my own as we clanked them together with a smile. "Me, too," she said.

She was quiet for a minute afterward while she looked around the room. Something seemed to be irritating her eyes because they got a little watery.

"Is there something in your eye, Aunt Esther? I think Nana has a magnifying glass over there." I stood up to fetch it. "I'll go get it for you."

"No, no … it's okay." She sniffed and wiped away the fallen tear. "I haven't told your mother this, but uh …" she stammered. "Um, I have breast cancer, too."

I was shocked. I suddenly felt years older than seven. It was like my soul instantly aged, like I was seventeen or something. "Oh … that's not good, right?"

"No, Grace … it's not good."

"Why haven't you told Momma?"

"Oh, I don't want to worry her. You should have seen how she took the news about your nana. It devastated her. The last thing I want to do, is make her upset like that ever again."

I thought about how sad Momma would be. She was already sad enough about losing her momma. She couldn't take much more grief around here, it seemed. "So, *that's* why you're always traveling and going to see new places."

I had an epiphany. It all made sense now.

She shrugged then said, "Pretty much."

"Because you're living."

"Yup, you got it."

❧ *Twenty-One* ❧
Football Injury

I had a new understanding of Aunt Esther. I guess we both had secrets. All we wanted was to protect our loved ones from feeling bad. I went into the open colorful cozy guest room where Aunt Esther was staying. I saw her extra pair of sandals tucked under the wood-framed bed. I liked the way her bed was made. The yellow pompom trimmed coverlet was pulled all the way up with a bunch of fluffy mismatched pillows resting along the headboard. Grownups liked having made beds, it seemed. It kind of made me want to go make my bed look as sophisticated.

I remembered that Aunt Esther was off doing something with Momma. I had come in here for something but couldn't remember what it was now. I decided to head on down to Nana's to get back to work. Before I went, I told Mazie about Aunt Esther's cancer and how she was living with it ... instead of dying because of it.

She was proud of Aunt Esther for being so strong. I was too. Sometimes strength isn't as obvious in some people. Take for instance, my papa, it was obvious by his muscles that he was strong but some people have a strong will, and they can overcome things with their attitude. That's what Aunt Esther was doing and what Nana had done.

I watched as Papa and Abel were throwing a football. I could tell my papa was not giving it his all. He was taking it easy on Abel who was small but mighty.

Papa smiled; he loved watching Abel run.

Abel had the funniest little gallop. It was like he was raised by horses because he literally trotted and galloped at high speed. He had enough energy to run all day and all night.

Papa threw a high whistler that I would have been scared to catch. I had jammed a thumb or two catching one of those footballs, but Abel had a knack for finding the right hand placement to gently allow for the ball to land harmlessly into his little palms. He was a natural, just like my papa.

"Heads up!" Abel called as he chucked the ball my way.

"No!" I called. I didn't want the ball to land in Mazie! I got up to stand in front of the puddle, blocking her from being hit. I stared as the ball whizzed over and set my focus on its spiraling motion, ready to catch it. It landed at a horizontal angle into my two awaiting hands with a sting.

"Ow! I don't want to play football. It always hurts my hands."

"Well, that was one heck of a catch if I do say so myself!" Papa seemed impressed. I chucked him the football then turned to go down to Nana's, but Papa ran to catch up with me.

"Where ya headed?" Papa asked as I was headed down to the woods.

"Nana's."

"Hold up for a second," he said as he gently put his hand on my shoulder, to make me stop.

"What for?" I asked looking up at him, but the glaring sun caused me to squint and look away.

He kneeled down to look me in the eye. Papa got the good eyes. His eyes were bluish green. They looked like the forest and the sky met in one spot—his eyes.

"It's a surprise," I said bashfully.

"Oh, I see," he said raising his one eyebrow and giving my belly a ticklish pinch.

"Yeah."

"Did I ever tell you that you are as pretty as a petunia?" Papa leaned in and pecked my cheek.

"Yes," I giggled.

"I did? Well, how about, did I ever tell you that you're cuter than an otter pup?"

"Yes," I giggled some more. I couldn't help

but love it when Papa made me feel special.

"I did?"

"Yes."

"Did I ever tell you that I love you from here to infinity?" Papa stretched out his arms all the way.

"Yup."

"Well, I'm gunna tell you again and again, okay?" he said while giving me a nuggle (that's what Nana called hugs and kisses) on my neck.

"Yes, it's okay with me if you tell me that every day, Papa," I said through a stream of giggles.

"Throw me the ball, Papa!" Abel called. Papa gave me a sweet smile then lofted the ball over to Abel as I went on my way.

⤳ *Twenty-Two* ⤳
Oh Deer!

While walking through the quiet woods, hairs stood up on my arms even though there was no sign of danger. I turned to check behind me as I walked. Apparently my hairs could sense presences before I could.

A tall white stag, with at least twenty points, on top of his enormous antlers, was standing still as a tree when I made eye contact with him. I couldn't believe what I was seeing! I felt like I had found a Unicorn or a Pegasus. Who would ever believe me if I told them about this completely white deer?

"Hi, magical Deerie!" I said, hoping to not spook it. He stomped his hoof. "It's okay, I won't hurtcha." I tried to ease his worry. He sniffed around and then blew a quick blast of air out of his nose. I held up my hands to let him know that he could trust me as I walked toward him.

He stood as if he was going to let me pet him, but just as my hand was about to touch his snowy hide, he leaped away.

He grunted as he bounded away. I listened to his hooves leaping and landing, disappearing deeper into the forest. I hoped I would see him again. He was so … so … I was having trouble finding the right words to describe him. None of them seemed spectacular enough. The best word I could think of was marvelous, no fascinating, or what about staggering?

As I was looking for the right word, a lady bug dropped onto my hand. At first I wasn't sure what kind of flying insect it was until she put her wings away and showed me her red, spotted shell. I carried her the rest of the way, but she flew off as I was about to turn the knob on Nana's front door.

I was nearly finished with all my projects by the end of the day and couldn't wait to give them away. It was almost dusk when Nana's door creaked open. Who was there? Probably Aunt Esther, I thought. I tidied up then went downstairs to find Hope looking around at Nana's pictures. She was standing with her hands clasped behind her back. She was wearing her pink overalls and her mahogany hair in two long braids.

"Hi, Hope," I greeted.

"Momma sent me here to fetch you. She needs some help with dinner."

"Okay, I was just about to go home anyway."

Hope closed the door behind us as we stepped out into a firefly foray. I always loved this time of day when the fireflies blinked all through the woods. Their strobes lit our path up the hill to our house.

"What is it that you are doing every day at Nana's?"

It was time I came clean to Hope, *but* I couldn't tell her everything. "Well, I'm planning a surprise."

"You won't tell me what it is?"

"You'll know soon enough."

"When?"

"At the party."

"What party?"

"The party I'm having to celebrate Nana's life," I said.

Hope seemed mystified. "Didn't we already have a funeral for her?"

"Yes, but that was because she died. It wasn't fun, and Nana liked to have fun."

Hope couldn't argue with that.

"Who's coming?" she asked.

"I'm going to invite all of Nana's friends and, of course, all of us, Aunt Esther Momma, Papa, you, and Abel."

"Does Momma know about this?"

"No! It's a surprise!"

"That's your big surprise?"

"Kind of," I coyly answered.

"That's going to be a big party. Who's helping you?"

I shrugged and said, "No one, yet."

As we walked, a small smile appeared on Hope's face. "Want some help?"

"Yes, but I don't know who to ask."

"Me, silly! I'll help!" Hope went from her normal seriousness to excitement in a flash. I hadn't seen this side of her in like … I tried to recall … ever. "What do you want me to do?"

What could I ask her to do? "Uh … let me think."

"How about I'll help you send out the invitations since your handwriting is a little hard to read."

"Hey!" I said but couldn't argue her point. Letters, words, and I didn't have the best relationship. Plus, Hope did have the neatest writing—even better than Momma's.

"Where is it going to be?" she asked.

"Nana's boogie barn."

"That's perfect! Okay, we need decorations, food, music, and punch."

I hadn't thought of all those things. Boy, was I glad Hope agreed to help me! Now this party would be extra great!

Twenty-Three
Invitations

We spent the next week handwriting the invitations. I did the artwork while Hope used her calligraphy pens to make them look extra neat and fancy. After they were ready, we took long walks handing out the invitations by hand.

We came to a house that was out of the ordinary in every way. It was in the center of town, surrounded by a brick library on one side and a white post office on the other. This house was a pink and green Victorian that looked magical with its daring color scheme. There was a large front porch that covered a set of rocking chairs, a porch swing, lots of beautifully arranged plants, and a dark magenta front door.

Hope rang the doorbell.

A dog started yapping like we were dangerous criminals. The door opened with a blast of vanilla frosting scent spilling out from the opening and a tiny Weiner dog with one eye sniffing us top to bottom, wagging his tail. He barked more, but it sounded like a greeting.

"Hush! Pinky, hush!" a pretty, pink-haired lady said. Hope handed her the invitation, introduced us, and said some other things while I tried to find the source of that delicious scent.

"My, my, Hope and Grace, aren't you two the most thoughtful girls! Why, I'd simply be delighted to come!" Miss Feekle, one of Nana's dancing ladies, said.

Miss Feekle sounded stuffed up when she spoke, but she didn't seem to have a cold. "Come on in, Hunnies, have a glass of lemonade, won't ya?"

"Actually we've," Hope started to say before I interrupted her and said, "Okay!"

"*This* is the *ladies* room, Hunnies, welcome!" she said as she ushered us into the space. Hope chuckled at the name.

Candles were lit around the house even though it wasn't dark, but they were responsible for the delicious deceptive scent.

Pinky stared at us cheerfully panting while we sipped pink lemonade in Miss Feekle's pink parlor. I guess Miss Feekle made an exception for Pinky in the *ladies* room.

There was pink everywhere. On the walls, pink striped wallpaper hung behind wreaths filled with dried pink flowers. The pink shag carpeting was super soft under our feet. We sat on a lovely pink velvet tufted couch that was next to a pair of fluffy pink bean bags. I wanted to flop onto them right away, but I restrained myself understanding the formality in our visit.

A pink glass chandelier lit the room for an extra pinker effect. I loved it and everything in this room, but Hope seemed to think otherwise judging from her facial expression. A bowl full of jellybeans was calling my name so I gladly chewed on a couple after Miss Feekle said, "Go right ahead, dear. That's why they're there!"

My jelly bean danced around in my mouth before my loose tooth popped out along with some blood.

Poop …

I hoped I didn't get on any of it on Miss Feekle's pink sofa. I thought I might cry after seeing the blood in my hand. Hope looked at me with horror springing from her face while Pinky barked at the commotion.

"Oh gosh!" Hope said as she grabbed me off the sofa and took me to the kitchen. Miss Feekle hushed Pinky then handed Hope a washcloth to clean me up. I felt bad. What if I messed up this nice lady's house?

Miss Feekle didn't look bothered. In fact, she said the nicest words that could have been said to me. "Well, look at that! You lost your tooth! Well, if that don't beat all! That's a good sign, so it's said. Now here's a silk satchel to wrap up that little ol' tooth. You're going to need it tonight under your pillow for the Tooth Fairy to come!"

Excitement spread through my circuits like

an electric boogaloo.

Miss Feekle refilled my glass of lemonade that I slurped up in an instant. Miss Feekle deserved a big thank you before we left which we were happy to oblige.

"I'll see y'all soon!" she called as we walked out of her driveway. "Good luck with that Tooth Fairy!"

When we walked into town, we found more of Nana's friends and invited them, too. By the end of the day, it seemed that we had invited close to, if not, the entire town of Apple Valley—even Dottie Doohinkley, who noticed my empty tooth slot right away.

"You be sure to gargle with salt water okay? You don't want to catch infection," she said, but Hope seemed to think her warning was unnecessary.

When we returned home, our excitement was still brimming. We told Aunt Esther to make sure Momma and Papa stayed away from the barn, and that she couldn't say a word about it or why.

After supper, Hope and I decorated the barn. We draped Nana's quilts around, stacked up hay bales, and put more quilts on them so loose straws wouldn't stick anyone. We hung more of Nana's favorite white twinkly lights and swept up the floor. A table topped with a cloth was put up to hold all of the food and drinks. After we had finished, we admired all of our hard work. The boogie barn looked magnificent. This party was going to be the best!

AND THE PURPLE PUDDLE

ເ∾ *Twenty-Four* ∾ວ
Pixie Nana

Right after I brushed my remaining teeth, I placed the special silk satchel that held my bloody tooth safely under my pillow. As I was lying in bed poking the empty tooth slot with my tongue, I looked around my starlit room imagining Nana's party. It was too bad that Nana couldn't be there to enjoy it because I knew she would have a blast scootin' and tootin' here and there, all around the boogie barn.

My thoughts began to sway with the music in my head. Before I knew it, I had drifted off to sleep.

Nana came into my bedroom flying like a Neverland pixie. She circled around the ceiling, went from the window to the closet, poked her nose close to my starry nightlight then landed on my bed with a twinkle.

I sat up. "Nana! You're here!"

"Of course I am, Grace!"

"Guess what?" I anxiously asked.

"What?"

"I'm having a party for you!"

"Oh!!!!" she squealed and flew up like a glowing spinning top. "I love parties!"

"I know. That's why Hope and I cleaned your barn and decorated it."

"You did?"

"Uh-huh!" I nodded.

"Can I see it?"

"Yes, let's go!"

Suddenly Nana's wings began to flutter and sparkle. Glitter dust floated all around as Nana picked me up and we flew over to her boogie barn.

We hovered inside before she gently let me down. She floated around the barn, noticing all the different decorations we had placed here and there. She lifted up one of the quilts and smelled it, rubbed her finger along the surfaces then silently nodded, congratulating us on our impeccable dusting.

"Spit Spot!" Nana affirmed. That was her term for cleaning to perfection.

"This is where all the food and drinks are going," I told her as I proudly stood in front of the table.

"That's a perfect spot! You and Hope did a great job! I couldn't have planned this party any better myself," Nana said proudly.

"There's only one thing left to do," I said.

"What's that?" Nana asked.

"DANCE!" I said.

"Oh! Okay, well then, let's dance!" Nana grabbed my hands as we weightlessly twisted, hopped, bopped, bobbed, and leaned to a magical melody. We danced all night long until we were both breathless.

"I think it's time for me to get you back to bed," Nana said.

"But, I'm not ready to say goodbye." After I said this, I realized that we were back in my bedroom, and Nana was sitting on my bed in the same spot as before we had flown over to the barn.

"You don't have to say goodbye, Grace."

"Then what should I say?"

"Just goodnight!" Nana leaned over to give me a kiss on my forehead.

"Oh!" I yawned. "Goodnight," I smiled sleepily as restful darkness returned to my room.

When I woke in the morning, I had the strangest happy feeling.

ᴗ *Twenty-Five* ᴗ

Free Money

Normally, I woke up slowly, but today I flew out of bed running for the bathroom mirror.

I searched my face. I knew it! I had gotten a new freckle right on my forehead! Nana *really was* an angel-kissing fairy! I stared at the everlasting lipstick, absolutely transfixed by its appearance.

I heard Abel call from down the hall,

"Ohhh! Look at all this money I found?"

"Money?" I repeated. I walked over to Abel who was standing near my bed holding a five-dollar bill.

"That's my money," I said unsurely, because I had never seen that money before. But I remembered putting my lost tooth under my pillow before bed but also thinking that that was a lot of money coming from the Tooth Fairy. Normally, I got some coins or loose change so a five-dollar bill was a big deal. Was it mine? It had to be mine, otherwise how would Abel have found it in my room?

"Finders keepers," Abel jokingly said but with a little seriousness mixed in. I wasn't about to let go of my free tooth money without a fight.

Abel took off running with his cape blowing, taking to the air. "Hey!" I cried out while chasing after his speedy little legs. He dashed, then darted, avoiding my grab. I started to panic thinking I would never get my five dollars back. My good morning was quickly unraveling.

"Give me back my money!" I screamed.

Momma came running up. "What's going on?" she asked while watching me chase Abel. I was too busy trying to catch him to answer. However, Momma caught me.

"Hey! He's getting away! He stole my Tooth Fairy money!" I urgently said while trying to wiggle out from her grip.

"Tooth Fairy money? Did you lose a tooth?" Momma asked, setting me down.

"Uh-huh," I said with tears about to spill.

Momma's face had a flash of guilt before she changed it back to her usual Momma face.

"Are you sure the Tooth Fairy came?" she asked, looking around, puzzled.

"Uh-huh, I lost my tooth yesterday and put it under my pillow, ask Hope."

"Why didn't you tell me you lost your tooth?" Momma asked.

"Why would I have to?" I wondered.

Momma cleared her throat. "Hope, can you come here?" Momma called.

After a few seconds, Hope opened the door of her room, poking out her sleepy head.

"Someone looks extra sleepy. Have you been up all night studying?" Momma asked.

"Um, not studying, but yes, I was up."

"What were you doing?" Momma asked.

"Just taking care of some things," Hope said coyly.

Momma seemed to understand what Hope was trying to tell her telepathically.

"Abel, you get back here right now and give Grace her money," Momma yelled.

"But finders keepers!" he tried to explain from his muffled hiding spot.

"Come out, come out, wherever you are," Papa summoned.

Abel reluctantly uncovered himself from the remnants of the blanket fort he had reconstructed in his bedroom then slowly walked over with the bill balled up in his fist.

"Okay, where did you find this?" Momma asked Abel.

"On the floor in Grace's room," he reluctantly confessed.

"Give it back to Grace," Papa ordered.

Abel handed over the wadded up bill then took off running. Papa jogged behind him after giving me a warm grin.

"Everything better now?" Momma bent

down to ask while wiping away a silly tear.

"Yeah, guess so." I unfolded the bill trying to straighten it, but it had been so tightly balled up, it wouldn't release the wrinkles easily. *It's ruined*, I thought.

"Come with me." Momma seemed to be able to read my mind because she brought me to the laundry/mudroom, got out the iron, plugged it in, waited for it to get hot, and then told me to iron it out.

I worked on it for a while until it was nice and crisp again. Momma sure was smart. I would have never thought that my five-dollar bill could have been restored.

From the laundry room, I overheard Hope and Momma talking quietly.

Hope said, "… from my birthday money that I had saved. I forgot to tell you that she had lost her tooth, and I knew she would be looking for it in the morning."

I walked into the kitchen and asked, "What are you talking about?"

"Oh, nothing," they said in unison.

I showed off my new, crisp, five-dollar bill. They *oohed* and *ahhed*. Abel and Papa came into the kitchen also *oohing* and *ahhing* about my neat ironing.

"Can I hold it?" Abel asked.

"No!" I said. I wasn't falling for that!

"Just kidding," he said. "But can I see your missing tooth?"

"Oh, yeah," I opened up my mouth then used my tongue to show him where my tooth used to be. He looked grossed out and fascinated all at once.

"I can't wait to lose my tooth! I'll be rich!" Abel said while wiggling a sturdy tooth. "Is this one loose?"

AND THE PURPLE PUDDLE

✍ *Twenty-Six* ✍

Nana's Cabin

The next day was dedicated to food preparations. Hope and I snuck away early to go to Nana's cabin. Aunt Esther was already there with all our necessary ingredients. I turned on some happy music as we got to work. The house warmed with the most delicious scents as I made Nana's special chocolate chip cookies. Hope made deviled eggs which were actually heavenly. Hope whipped up the yolks like no one ever could. She topped them with a tiny slice of pickle, too. Aunt Esther made noodle salad, baked beans, and chicken wings. Plus, she made the best red berry punch I have ever tasted. Sweet tart apple berry mixed with sugar is what I called it after taking a spoonful. It had just the right amount of sugar and everyone knows that sugar makes tastiness (at least that's what Nana said). Yes, of course we made lemonade made from freshly squeezed lemons, water, and sugar.

As we stepped onto the porch to bring the dishes over to the boogie barn, a rusty cardinal was sitting on the porch railing. It twitched then flew up and away. I looked up as we were walking, watching the bird land in the scrubby tree near the barn. By the way it flew, a strange thought occurred to me ... I wondered if that could be Nana? But when Hope hurried me along, I dismissed my "duh-lusion".

∽∾ • ∽∾

As the sun went down, the fireflies came out to greet everyone arriving to Nana's party. In these parts, folks don't show up to a party without a covered dish so the food table became stuffed with a variety of meats, casseroles, gelatins, salads of all sorts, puddings, pies, cookies and cakes. It was quite a sight. Everyone mingled together nicely, asking about each other's loved ones, as usual.

When it looked like everyone had arrived, Hope and I ran up to get Momma, Papa, and Abel.

"Momma! Papa! We have a surprise for you down at Nana's boogie barn," I said.

"Yeah," Hope said with as much enthusiasm as her voice could muster.

Momma was busy being busy as usual and didn't have time to come, but Papa could sense our despair at her brushoff.

He helped us by gently taking her hand saying, "Dear, I think it might be really important what these girls want to show you. Could you just take a little second to see what it is?"

Momma's heart melted when Papa talked to her so sweetly then she looked at us girls and Abel, who had the cutest little puppy dog expression on his face.

"Okay, let me just get cleaned up a bit."

That was probably a good idea considering Momma still had some flour on her face from the biscuits she had made. We anxiously waited in the living room for her and Papa to come down. Her hair was brushed and her face was washed, but her clothes were plain, like always—a long restricting skirt and a white unfitting shirt—not good dancing clothes.

I knew that if she wore clothes that fit right, she would look much better. I knew because I saw her in a bathing suit when we'd go to the lake or waterfalls, and she looked a lot better than most other moms. Momma didn't know she was still young and pretty.

I made an announcement to everyone. "Before we go, I have some presents I'd like to give to you but you have to promise that you will wear them. No exceptions," I said as I gave Momma a stern stare.

Momma and Papa looked at each other like they were unsure.

"Do you promise?" I asked.

"Yes," Papa said first, but Momma still seemed skeptical.

"Momma, please. I made something special, just for you," I pleaded.

"Well, what is it?" she asked.

"You have to promise first!" I wasn't falling for any of that trickery.

She looked to Papa who gave her a stern look then said, "Okay, I promise but it can't be anything ridiculous." She tried to leave a little wiggle room. I wasn't falling for that either.

"No, you have to promise, no matter what."

She glanced over at Papa again for some guidance, but he only gestured for her to promise. She huffed. "Okay, I promise."

"Good, but first I will give Abel *his* gift."

"I have a present? Oh boy! I love presents," he giggled.

I handed him a package wrapped in newspaper. I didn't have enough money to get real wrapping paper *and* plan the party so I made do. He ripped it open faster than a raccoon tearing through trash.

He pulled out a "real" super hero cape with a purple "A" embroidered in the center. The cloak was mostly red alongside purple trim with Velcro that secured around the neck. He looked at it for a second then tore off his ratty old towel like a superhero would in order to put on his fancy new cape then zoomed around the house making swooshing sounds. I think he liked it.

"Thank you, Grace!" Abel said while zooming.

"Here's yours, Hope," I said as I handed my gift to her.

"For me?" She seemed shocked.

"Yup, just for you."

She unwrapped a pumpkin-colored space suit like I had seen other astronauts wear. It wasn't exactly like a "real" space suit, but it was as close as I could get it to be, patches and all. She was speechless but her mouth was wide open. She just kept making strange sounds until she said, "I'll be right back!"

Quicker than a cheetah, Hope returned with her suit on—it fit her just right! She looked ready for takeoff! "I love it, Grace! How did you ever do this? It's perfect!" She gave me a big hug—the first hug she'd given to me since I could remember.

"Here's yours, Papa!"

"For me?"

"Yes! Hurry up! We have to go soon!" I said looking over at the late time on the clock.

"Oh, well, let me just, uh ..." he fumbled with the package until he unwrapped a football jersey with his number seventeen on it from high-school. I made it to match Momma's present so you'd know they were together. Without going anywhere, Papa ripped off his t-shirt then slipped on the jersey that made him look twenty years younger.

He looked so proud while Abel called out, "Catch!" as he threw a football to Papa.

"Hey! No ball-throwing in the house," Momma said.

"This one's for you Momma, but you'll have to be blindfolded. Hope and I will help you put it on in your bedroom."

"I'm not so sure about this," she skeptically warned.

"Don't worry Momma! Everyone else loves their gifts, you will, too. I'm sure!" I said.

"Yeah, do as she says," Papa said and gave me a big wink.

I gave him a big wink too as we headed upstairs.

As we were standing in front of Momma's big mirror, Hope put a blindfold on Momma. "I don't like this! What are you two up to?"

"Take off your clothes," I said.

"Poodle Poo! No, I will not."

"It's just for a second so I can put you in something better."

Momma eventually stopped resisting and let us dress her. When we were finished, Hope ran downstairs to get Papa and Abel, who were instructed to wait at the door, silently.

When we removed Momma's blindfold, she gasped. Momma was wearing a dancing dress—a dress she could boogie in. It had ruffles on top of ruffles and it fit just right. I had made it out of one of Nana's old dancing dresses but made it more suited for Momma. She stared at herself then sat back on her bed with a couple of tears poised to drop.

"Momma, do you not like it?" I asked.

"No, Grace …" she sniffed. "I love it." She was quiet for a couple of seconds then she turned to Papa and said, "It's just that I don't have anywhere to wear such a fine dress."

Boy, was she in for a surprise. "Just wear it

here for tonight," I said.

"Okay." She stood back up, looked at herself in the mirror, gingerly twirling the ruffles back and forth.

"You ... look stunning Ruth—not a day older than when I first laid eyes on you. Come on, let me take you for a walk." Papa held out his arm for Momma to grab. She placed her hand within his protective embrace as they started to go. He turned around to say, "Come on, kids, let's all go on a walk in our new outfits made by **THE AMAZING GRACE NEWTON.**"

We all scurried out of the house. I looked back at our living treehouse. In the evening, it looked so cozy with the amber light glowing from the windows and doors. The smokeless chimney stack waited to warm our wintery nights. The black shutters framed the wooden windows offering protection, if necessary. If I didn't live here or get to see my home every day, I'd think it was enchanted.

The five of us Newtons clomped down the mountain road with excitement for many reasons. We were all wearing new clothes, except for me. I was wearing a newish dress that was pretty enough. My family each got a gift, but what I got was a feeling, the feeling of giving, and it felt super good to give.

Momma seemed relaxed in her new dress. She even walked with a little sass. Papa looked so strong in his jersey while Abel looked *super*, especially as he zoomed around to and fro in front of us because we were always too slow. Hope walked proudly, like she was getting ready to board the space shuttle. It's funny what an outfit can do for your confidence.

As we came closer to Nana's boogie barn, I could hear the party already well underway. Smith and Wesson were outside doing wheelies on Luke and Han. I waved as they pedaled over to us to say hi.

"Hi, guys!" I said.

Cars were parked here and there; Momma looked confused.

"What's going on here? Someone needs to tell these people that this is private property." She pointed to the sign painted with a couple of rascally bunnies that read, ***Hippity Hoppity, Get Off My Property***.

"Let's go in and see what's going on," Papa

said as he looked over to me to give me a big wink.

Momma looked suspicious, but her reluctance came too late. The barn doors swung open as Aunt Esther and Alice ushered us all in. Everyone clapped making a big ruckus before they were hushed by Mr. Skwertz who asked for everyone's attention. He cleared his throat before he spoke into the microphone.

"I'd like to thank you all for coming, especially The Newtons. Andromeda Markarian was a much loved and respected lady in this here community as evidenced by all of you showing up to celebrate her life. But none of us would be here if it wasn't for little Grace Newton who planned this whole thing so we could all dance together—the way Andromeda would have liked it. Every single one of you was important to her and vice versa. Now, we are going to sing some songs, eat some delicious food, and, most importantly, dance!"

Everyone cheered before Mr. Skwertz hushed them once again to say, "But to start the evening off right, would you all please help me welcome Mr. Lumen and Mrs. Ruth Newton up here to the dance floor to begin our first dance."

Everyone clapped again, making way for Momma and Papa to walk to the dance floor. At first Momma was hesitant, but Mr. Skwertz said, "C'mon you two, show these folks how to move, and don't act like you don't know how to dance. I was at your wedding and saw you guys cut the dance floor like a couple of Hollywood movie stars."

Momma blushed then let Papa lead her to the center of the crowd. The music began with something nice, and slow, but when my Papa brought Momma into his embrace, it was quick—the crowd roared.

Momma's dress twirled the way I knew it would. I could tell she liked it. He pushed her away then brought her in before dipping her slowly. His forehead found hers as they stared into each other's eyes.

They must really like each other, I thought. He lifted her back up then they glided around the circle until the crowd closed in on them, dancing as well.

Hope and I watched as the party we had

worked so hard to plan was happening. Tater Skwertz, who was at my Nana's funeral, offered me his hand. I wasn't sure what he was trying to give me so I waited for him to speak.

"Wanna dance?"

I looked over to Hope who nodded quickly, telling me to get out there.

"Okay," I said and took his hand. At first it felt weird, especially when I spotted Smith and Wesson snickering at us. I stuck my tongue out at them then shrugged my shoulders.

"Don't pay attention to them, just have fun and dance," Tater said.

He was right. Eventually dancing *was* fun, and we were bouncing around, jumping like a couple of bullfrogs with absolutely no dancing skills at all. Hope and Abel were doing some sort of swing dance, but Abel was the only one getting swung around. He was giggling and so was I. Smith and Wesson even got into the mix—the music was that captivating.

Everyone was having a grand time. There wasn't a single wallflower. I was surprised that Miss Doohinkley wasn't trying to sell any of her stinky lotions and makeup. She was too busy trotting along with a happy man being led by her.

Nearly everyone stayed well into the night. When the party was over, I realized I hadn't eaten any of the party food. I was too busy having fun.

It was time to clean up—the not fun part. Momma told us not to worry … that we could take care of it in the morning. I was too tired and happy to argue.

We Newtons walked home together. Along the way, I noticed the silver moon smiling down on us as a star streamed across the sky.

"Wow!" Hope and I said at the same time.

"Wow what?" Abel asked looking all around.

"A shooting star!" we said, again in unison.

"Oh, man!"

"Tell me your wish Abel, and I'll wish for you," I said, because all of my wishes had already come true.

Abel thought for a second then whispered in my ear, "Um, I wish I had a loose tooth."

I giggled. "You sure that's what you want to wish for?" I asked.

"Yup!" he said sure of his request.

I stopped to concentrate on his wish then told him that it was done. Abel got excited causing him to run the rest of the way home.

∽ *Twenty-Seven* ∾
One Last Thing

I was too tired to make myself a snack but too hungry to go to bed when Aunt Esther and Alice, Aunt Esther's traveling friend, came in with plates of food just for us.

"In case you didn't get to eat at your own party, we brought these for you."

I couldn't have been more grateful as I gobbled up those delectable goodies like an aardvark.

"Oh! I have something for you, Aunt Esther and Alice!" I just remembered that I hadn't given my gift to them.

"Oh you didn't have to give us anything," Aunt Esther said as I was tiredly jogging upstairs to get it.

I handed them a hunk wrapped in newspaper. They looked at me like I'd just given them the best thing ever. "Open it!" I said.

They unwrapped a pillow in the shape of their RV—well, it was supposed to be in the shape of Ol' Tex.

"Is this what I think it is?" Aunt Esther asked.

I nodded. "It's so you'll always have a place to rest your head when you're on the road."

"Wow Grace, you really are somethin'," Alice said marveling at my craftsmanship.

The grandfather clock chimed over and over again in the living room.

"All right kiddos! It's 11:00 PM, way past beddy-bye time," Papa said.

"Oh, I forgot something, Papa. I'll be right back," I called as I scuttled out from the screen door accidentally slamming it.

"Don't slam …" Momma started to say and then finished with "Oh, whatever …"

Before I could go to bed, I had to go outside to see Mazie. As soon as I got closer, I could see her in the pale moonlight. She yawned at the same time I did.

"Well, how did it go?" she asked sleepily.

I tried to come up with the best words to describe the evening's festivities but all I could think to say was, "It was amazing!"

Aunt Eva's
Panekaka Recipe

4 eggs
1 ½ cup of milk
1 cup flour
½ stick of butter, melted in frying pan
dash of salt

Beat up eggs; beat in milk; beat in flour; add melted
butter and dash of salt.

Pour batter into heated pan and make the batter spread
over the bottom of the pan.

When the batter looks a little bubbly and not too wet,
flip the pancake over and cook the other side.

Fold the pancake twice to form a squareish pancake.

Serve with honey, syrup, apple sauce, whipped cream,
berries or other topping like peanut butter and molasses.

Get ready for a
new adventure in
Amazing Grace Newton and The RV Trip!

It was barely dawn when Aunt Esther quietly padded into my bedroom. I was afraid the time for her to leave would come before I was ready. I didn't want to say goodbye.

"Are you leaving?" I sleepily asked.

"I am, yes, very soon."

My face turned upside down. "No, I don't want you to go," I softly pleaded as I rolled around in my sheets.

"Well, Grace, how would you like to come along with us, this time?" she asked.

My eyes shot open!

Throwing away the covers, I sat up in a dither. All my life, I had always wanted to go camping, or RVing, or whatever you called it. "Could I?"

"If you want to?"

"Yes! I want to. Is everyone else coming, too?"

"I think it's just going to be you kids, Alice, and me."

"Not Momma and Papa?"

"I think they could use some alone time, don't you?"

After a few moments of thought, I said, "Yeah, they do."

Aunt Esther patted my leg and said, "Well, if we're going to get going, we gotta get going!"

I threw off the rest of my covers and started to get ready. "I'll be ready in a flash!"

About the Author

N. Jane Quackenbush is a graduate of Palm Beach Atlantic University. She lives in an *Amazing* house filled with kitties and strange art in St. Augustine, FL. After a family trip to North Carolina, Ms. Quackenbush was inspired by the peaceful landscape and the wholesome  nature of the area. Amazing Grace Newton personifies the overwhelming emotions such inspirational settings produce.

You can also stay in touch with N. Jane Quackenbush on Facebook.

N. Jane Quackenbush has also written the following Children's Picture Books:
The Rocket Ship Bed Trip
The Pirate Ship Bed Trip
The Afternoon Moon

Middle Grade Books:
The Children's Horrible House
Return to The Children's Horrible House
Escape from The Children's Horrible House

If you enjoyed reading *Amazing Grace Newton and The Purple Puddle*, please leave a review.

51104681R00129

Made in the USA
Columbia, SC
18 February 2019